The Martial Arts Business Arena

Investment, Politics, Profit

An Anthology of Articles from the *Journal of Asian Martial Arts*

Compiled by Michael A. DeMarco, M.A.

Disclaimer
Please note that the authors and publisher of this book are not responsible in any manner whatsoever for any injury that may result from practicing the techniques and/or following the instructions given within. Since the physical activities described herein may be too strenuous in nature for some readers to engage in safely, it is essential that a physician be consulted prior to training.

All Rights Reserved
No part of this publication, including illustrations, may be reproduced or utilized in any form or by any means, electronic or mechanical, including photocopying, recording, or by any information storage and retrieval system (beyond that copying permitted by sections 107 and 108 of the US Copyright Law and except by reviewers for the public press), without written permission from Via Media Publishing Company.

Warning: Any unauthorized act in relation to a copyright work may result in both a civil claim for damages and criminal prosecution.

Copyright © 2016 by
Via Media Publishing Company
941 Calle Mejia #822
Santa Fe, NM 87501 USA
E-mail: md@goviamedia.com

All articles in this anthology were originally
published in the *Journal of Asian Martial Arts*.
Listed according to the table of contents for this anthology:

Friman, H.R. (1996), Vol. 5, No. 3, pp. 10-19
Ko, Y.J. (2003), Vol. 12, No. 2, pp. 8-19
Ko, Y.J., & Yang, J.B. (2008), Vol. 17, No. 4, pp. 8-15
Tharp, A. (2012), Vol. 21, No. 1, pp. 56-71

Book and cover design by Via Media Publishing Company
Edited by Michael A. DeMarco, M.A.

Cover illustration
Photograph of uniform and black belt
courtesy of www.iStock.com

ISBN: 978-1893765-36-8

www.viamediapublishing.com

contents

iv **Preface**
by Michael DeMarco, M.A.

CHAPTERS

1 **Blinded by the Light: Politics and Profit in the Martial Arts**
by H. Richard Friman, Ph.D.

13 **Martial Arts Marketing: Putting the Customer First**
by Yong Jae Ko, Ph.D.

23 **The Globalization of Martial Arts:
The Change of Rules for New Markets**
by Yong-jae Ko, Ph.D. and Jin-bang Yang, Ph.D.

37 **Nihonto: A Legal Perspective on
Japanese Swords and Their Intrinsic Value**
by Andrew Tharp, Ph.D.

52 **Index**

preface

Martial art business-related aspects are found at the base level in individual schools and mushroom to a global level in international organizations. This anthology includes writings by professionals who offer information and insights into the financial side of the martial arts. Chapters focus on related practical matters as profit, politics and investment.

In the first chapter, Dr. Richard Friman asks: If the martial arts are supposed to offer paths to personal growth and enlightenment, why are they, in practice, plagued with displays of rampant egos, politics, and battles over turf by their practitioners? The experience of instruction in the United States suggests that the pursuit of the arts is becoming lost in the pursuit of profit.

The next chapter by Dr. Yong Jae Ko presents the evolution of the martial arts industry into a global consumer products industry and examines the application of modern business techniques on this industry, with a particular focus on marketing strategy. It also discusses future opportunities and challenges facing the martial arts industry, and offers helpful suggestions.

In the following chapter, Dr. Ko and coauthor Dr. Jin Bin Yang discuss the global expansion and integration of Asian martial arts. Such factors as sportification and standardization are closely examined as significant driving forces for the growth of the martial arts industry. This chapter also examines important issues influencing the development and the martial arts' industry future growth.

The final chapter by Andrew Tharp presents the history that influenced the value of Japanese swords as works of art. The Japanese have created a legal system that has preserved their historical weapons in a way no other society has done. Historical sources and current statutes will show how the Japanese created a monopoly that successfully conserved their culture for future generations. Although this Japanese phenomenon is extraordinary, it also serves to show possibilities for those interested in investing in weaponry from other cultures and augments our appreciation of militaria for their aesthetics.

Reading this anthology will help martial art students better understand differences between traditional schools and those that focus solely on profit. Owners can deepen their business acumen and utilize information provided in these chapters to shape their schools' program. Of course many are influenced by martial art organizations that may be established on a local level, national or international. As an addition to your regular studies of martial art techniques and traditions, the information you'll find here can certainly broaden one's view of the martial arts as a business arena.

Michael A. DeMarco, Publisher
Santa Fe, New Mexico
October 2016

bionotes

- **H. Richard Friman, Ph.D.** is s Eliot Fitch Professor for International Studies, Professor of Political Science, and Director of the Center for Transnational Justice at Marquette University, Milwaukee, Wisconsin. His current research focuses on the intersection of the licit and illicit global economies. He earned his Ph.D. in government from Cornell University. Dr. Friman has over forty years of training in the martial arts in both the United States and Japan. During 1994-95, he was a visiting Fulbright Scholar with the National Research Institute of Police Science of the National Police Agency in Tokyo, Japan.

- **Yong-jae Ko, Ph.D.** is an assistant professor of the sport management program at University of Florida. He has been involved in numerous research projects that relate to consumer behavior and event marketing in the context of sport and martial arts. He routinely serves on various committees and advisory boards in national and international sport organizations. He has over twenty-eight years of teaching and coaching experiences in taekwondo and holds a 5th-dan black belt degree.

- **Andrew Tharp, Ph.D.** holds a bachelor's of science in business from the Indiana University Kelley School of Business, and a Certificate in Martial Arts from the Indiana University School of Health, Physical Education, and Recreation. In addition, he received his Doctor of Jurisprudence from the Indiana University Maurer School of Law. He earned his Moniteur d'Escrime (sabre) from the United States Fencing Coaches Association and the Académie d'Armes Internationale in 2007. His primary focus in his undergraduate martial arts work was weapon based combat. The senior fencing instructor for Indiana University, Andrew, is also an avid sword collector, and has published articles on sword collecting, western martial arts.

- **Jin-bang Yang, Ph.D.** is a professor in Yong In University's Taekwondo Competition Program in S. Korea. He received his Ph.D. from University of North Carolina at Greensboro (Physical Education) in 1996. His seminal work on taekwondo history is regarded as the highest impact scholarly work in this subject. Dr. Yang has been working for Kukkiwon and Korea Taekwondo Association as a director and executive member. In 1990s, Dr. Yang introduced taekwondo to many Chinese when he was a faculty member of Beijing University. Today, he is known as "the Father of Taekwondo in China."

Notes

chapter 1

**Blinded by the Light:
Politics and Profit in the Martial Arts**

by H. Richard Friman, Ph.D.

According to scholars and practitioners, the study of martial arts such as karate offers an array of physical and mental benefits. At the core of the arts, lies a path to personal growth and enlightenment. For those who walk the path, considerations based on personal ego fade over time and are replaced by the internalization of discipline, self-respect, integrity, loyalty, and commitment to learning. Conflict and confrontation, instead of being sought, are avoided by the martial artist whenever possible. Violence is turned to only as a last resort (Funakoshi, 1981; A Way to Stop, 1993: 114).

This chapter explores a growing paradox. If the martial arts are supposed to offer paths to personal growth and enlightenment, why are they, in practice, plagued with displays of rampant egos, politics, and battles over turf by their practitioners? The experience of karate instruction in the United States suggests that the pursuit of the arts is becoming lost in the pursuit of profit.

The Path & the Problem

Martial arts as currently practiced in the United States includes an array of styles with roots ranging from countries of East and Southeast Asia to, more recently, those of Europe and Africa. Yet, the extent to which each style advocates a combative system, broader philosophy, or sportification through formal competition differs. The relative importance of these characteristics within a given style has also tended to change over time (Urban, 1967: 143; Yamaguchi, 1972: 6).

For example, as argued by D. Draeger and R. Smith, the Japanese martial arts styles of the twentieth century are largely removed from the classical combat systems as developed 1,000 years earlier. The combat systems were focused on "battlefield use" such that the exercise of blows resulted in injury or death. Changing political and social conditions of the mid-eighteenth century led to the emergence of newer martial ways (*budo*) incorporating the idea of practice as a path to personal enlightenment.

Although a limited number of martial arts styles can still trace their roots to the earlier combat systems, modern budo arts tend to emphasize enlightenment and, increasingly, a sport orientation (Draeger and Smith, 1980: 90-93; Donohue, 1994: 41-42, 49). This combination was the most common version of Japanese and Okinawan karate styles that began to make their way to the United States during the 1950's and 1960's. In the United States over the past several decades, however, the trend towards karate as sport rather than martial way appears to have become the rule rather than the exception.

As argued by Draeger, the shift in Japan towards sportification of the arts emerged with the introduction of free-sparring in the mid-1930's by Gichin Funakoshi, and the "competitions and championships" introduced by his successors in the Shotokan style during the 1950's. The emphasis on more competition-oriented techniques and the phasing out of traditional techniques such as low kicks and throws, through the activities of Shotokan-based Japan Karate Association (JKA), proved to be popular especially with younger Japanese. Draeger posits that, faced with the possibility for losing potential students to the growing JKA "sport style," other budo styles began "to follow similar techniques" (Draeger, 1974: 133-34). In this context, technical proficiency and its ties to the prestige of rankings and championships increasingly became the focus of many karate practitioners (Draeger and Smith, 1980: 93-94). Moreover, the relative influence of karate systems increasingly became a function of organizational ties and numbers of affiliated training halls (*dojo*) and students rather than the effectiveness or enlightenment dynamics of the art.

In 1964, six of the most influential karate associations and three national federations moved to consolidate karate within Japan by establishing the Federation of All Japan Karate-do Organizations (FAJKO). The JKA (Shotokan), Goju-kai (Japanese Goju-ryu under Gogen Yamaguchi), Wado-kai (Wado-ryu), Rembo-kai, Rengo-kai, and Shoto-kai (Shito-ryu) comprised the member associations. Organizations of colleges, workers, and the Self-Defense Forces (SDF) comprised the member federations (Draeger, 1974: 135-36). Yet, the consolidation was more important from the standpoint of organization and influence than any meeting of the minds on the common standard for karate-do.

The FAJKO's membership has shifted only slightly over the years—the high school students federation replacing the SDF and the inclusion of the Kyokushinkai style (under Masutatsu Oyama) (Corcoran, 1994: 374). The high school shift appears to reflect the organization's emphasis on the linkage to the youth market while the inclusion of Kyokushinkai reflects the incorporation of perhaps the strongest outside challenger to the FAJKO.

Estimates of the total number of karate styles and organizations in Japan are difficult at best and subject to interpretation. For example, Draeger posits the existence of over 100 different forms of karate while Funakoshi contends that perhaps only two or three distinct styles exist, other styles often reflecting "alterations due to poor mastery of techniques or ability, forgetting, or blending of tiny pieces of the arts" (Draeger and Smith, 1980: 140; Funakoshi, 1988: 28). By the early 1960's, Oyama's integration of Chinese, Korean, and Japanese styles into Kyokushinkai had produced a combative version of karate. In contrast to the sport-focused trend within the JKA, participants in Oyama's tournaments were required to demonstrate proficiency in breaking techniques as a prerequisite to competition, and sparring matches tended to end in either "knockout or surrender" rather than decisions based on points. The growing interest among Japanese in Kyokushinkai and its direction led Draeger to observe in a 1974 publication that Oyama's "popularity with Japanese Karate-do officials is not great" (Draeger, 1974: 134-35).

Although Oyama had trained with Funakoshi and Yamaguchi and had won the All-Japan Karate Championship in 1947, the Kyokushin organization was not initially incorporated into the FAJKO. The reasons for this omission are not clear. Possible explanations include a combination of stylistic differences, Oyama's Korean heritage (his having immigrated to Japan in 1938), and, as Jay Gluck suggests, an "unsavory reputation" stemming from his Korean patriotism in the turbulence of postwar Japan (Gluck, 1962: 12-13). However, the style's growing popularity and the number of competitive Japanese Kyokushin fighters created a force within Japanese karate that became too big for the FAJKO to ignore. The Kyokushin association's marketing efforts continue to be impressive. These include sponsorship of prestigious national and international championships and extensive media coverage (magazines, books, videos, and television specials) of the association's events and activities.

The Politics

If organizational disputes in Japan are often based on attracting numbers, the issue in the United States appears to be generating profit. The initial entry of karate to the United States followed various paths. During the late-1940's and early 1950's, for example, the U.S. Air Force began a series of programs relying on instructors (in some cases brought in from Japanese colleges) to introduce the arts of karate and judo to Americans stationed in Japan, Okinawa, and Korea (Haines, 1969: 137-38). Service personnel and other Americans exposed to the arts while abroad (such as Peter Urban, Goju-ryu; Robert Trias, Shotokan) became one source of instruction when they returned to the United States. Other paths introducing the arts to the United States took place through Hawaii with the blending of Japanese and Chinese arts into Kosho-ryu Kempo by James Mitose and his student William Chow (in turn, the instructor of Ed Parker). Taking advantage of growing interest in the arts, Japanese karate practitioners also came to the United States to instruct in styles such as Shotokan (Tsutomu Oshima, 1956; Hidetaka Nishiyama, 1959), Goju-ryu (Gosen Yamaguchi, 1962; and Gosei Yamaguchi, 1964), and Shito-ryu (Demura Fumio, 1965).

Bruce Haines argues that the key turning point in the development of the arts in the United States came with the dispute over which associations would gain Amateur Athletic Union (AAU) sanction of karate during the mid-1960's (Haines, 1969: 138-59). From 1961 through the 1970's, amateur sports in the United States became a battleground between the AAU and organizations such as the National Collegiate Athletic Association (NCAA) and the U.S. Track and Field Federation. The debate was often couched in terms of a dispute over the definition and philosophy of amateurism. However, the larger issues at stake were policy control, access to the Olympics, and, by the later-1960's, the lucrative issue of television rights. Mediators ranging from General MacArthur, congressional and executive branch officials, and representatives of the U.S. Olympic Committee all sought to resolve the issue.[1] For the relatively new karate organizations in the United States in this context, AAU sanction offered legitimacy, influence, and potential access to the association's network and population base.

Seeking sanction, associations under Parker, Oshima, and Korean martial artist Jhoon Rhee attempted to "unite U.S. karate factions and to fuse karate into American amateur athletics." However, competing claims emerged from organizations, including the Midwest-based American Karate Association and those established by Nishiyama (the All American Karate Association [AAKA], affiliated with the FAJKO), and Trias (U.S. Karate Association, USKA). By the late-1960's, however, efforts to form a unified proposal to the AAU had become deadlocked. A five-hour meeting of association representatives held in St. Louis broke down over the issue of who would be the leader of a united U.S. karate organization. Although largely a figurehead position, the association representatives, with few exceptions, either wanted it or refused to accept others holding it. In short, the relevancy of unification under AAU sanction faded as karate in the United States became increasingly distinguished by associations refusing to recognize each other, splits between groups led by Japanese instructors and those with non-Japanese instructors, and splits among Japanese groups themselves (Haines 1967: 137-38, 159).[2]

The American experience during this period was similar to events taking place on the international level. Peter Urban, for example, notes that profit considerations had led to an international dispute over official sanction and control over karate between Japanese, Okinawan, Korean, European, and United Stated organizations (Urban, 1967: 143). Roughly thirty years later, such national and international disputes show no signs of abating. Instead, the financial stakes and, in turn, the intensity of the disputes have increased. The initial experiment of including taekwondo into the Seoul Olympics increased the stakes in the domestic and international debates. For example, the mid-1980's saw a wave of centralization efforts among karate associations seeking the Olympic access. This trend led to the prominence of organizations such as the World Union of Karate-do Organizations and the designation of the USA Karate Federation (USAKF) as its American counterpart. The politics of these organizational shifts, however, continued following Seoul.

In July, 1992, the International Olympic Committee (IOC) "removed [the World Union] . . . as the international federation for amateur karate." In turn, the U.S. Olympic Committee (USOC) in June, 1993, removed the USAKF as the "national governing body for sport karate." The USOC decision noted that in the absence of the World Union, the USAKF was "unnecessary." However, the decision also appeared to reflect disputes and maneuvering by competing associations such as the AAU and the International Traditional Karate Federation. Both associations cited the USAKF's exclusionary and discriminatory politics against competing organizations and non-USAKF groups (USAKF Denied, 1994: 10-11).

In 1994, the International Olympic Committee formally accepted taekwondo as a full Olympic sport for the Sydney games in 2000. Unsurprisingly, the political maneuvering and repositioning for access has already begun. In 1995, for example, the USAKF had become a member (along with the USA National Karate-do Federation, and the American Amateur Karate Federation) of U.S. Karate Incorporated (U.S. Karate Inc., 1995: 107).

The politics of competing associations has also been affected by their proliferation. Since the 1960's, the explosion in the sheer number of competing associations and their affiliates within the United States has been staggering. The summer, 1995, issue of the U.S. martial arts marketing guide, *The Black Book*, for example, contains ten pages of major American associations. John Corcoran's extensive *Martial Arts Sourcebook* offers almost fifty pages of listings, twelve pages for the United States alone. The pages of martial arts magazines such as *Black Belt* reveal a partially overlapping array of additional organizations and associations with common mantras offering relief from politics, free black-belt testing or recognition, status, and opportunities for competition.

In addition to the organizations and associations discussed above, the major association lists include the United Fighting Arts Federation, Black Karate Federation, the American Independent Taekwondo/Karate Instructors Federation, the Professional Karate Association, the Professional Karate League, and the North American Sport Karate Association. Within taekwondo, comparable organization and politics have played out among what some call the big three and their international affiliates: the American Taekwondo Association and the World Taekwondo Union; U.S. Taekwondo Union and and the World Taekwondo Federation; and the U.S. Taekwando Federation and the International Taekwando Federation (Stephan, 1996: 50-58).

The Stakes

The surge in politics in the arts reflects a concurrent increase in the financial stakes involved. Over the past thirty years, karate instruction and tournament competition in the United States have become distinguished more by their business characteristics than by promotion of a martial way. These trends have been accelerated by the growing popularity of martial arts in American culture (Skidmore, 1991: 129-48). Since the wave of interest following the Bruce Lee films of the early 1970's, the martial arts in American popular culture have been influenced by two broad tracks: the martial arts action film and television genre aimed at children. It is this latter track—illustrated by the successive waves of interest among children and their parents sparked by the *Karate Kid* films and characters such as the *Teenage Mutant Ninja Turtles* and *(Mighty Morphin) Power Rangers*—that has had the most serious ramifications.

By 1995, karate instruction in the United States had become a $1.5 billion annual business, its growth having doubled since 1990 (Ferguson, 1995: 138-42). Instruction is increasingly distinguished by an emphasis on large volume enrollments, binding contracts (ranging from a few months to several years), and national chains of training halls (at times located in shopping malls). For example, the chain Martial Arts America has seen the number of its affiliated dojo in the United States and Canada increase from 9,000 to 16,000 since 1990. The dojo range in size from those with 65-70 students that "barely get by" to what the organization sees as more viable dojo of 150 students (Ferguson, 1995: 142).

Marketing programs, often costing hundreds of dollars, offer books and training seminars for instructors on how to boost enrollment and profits.

Promotion companies such as Global Financial, Educational Funding Company, Martial Arts Marketers Association, American Management Services, and Triad Enterprises advertise their services in martial arts magazines. In addition, martial arts billing and collections agencies (who for a percentage offer to make the former student honor the financial obligation) make sure that the instructor does not have to spend valuable time enforcing contracts. For example, United Professionals Inc. of Florida "collected $18 million" in 1994 as a billing agent for only 480 schools (Ferguson, 1995: 142).

The business of karate, by its very nature, encourages a shift away from the idea of the arts as path to enlightenment. From a business standpoint, high-volume student enrollments are necessary to offset the costs of high-profile locations and equipment (such as state-of-the-art weight machines) and to generate profit. Enrollment-to-space ratios are best served by catering to children rather than adults. Simply put, children are physically smaller. More paying students can be accommodated at any given training session. The emphasis on children is revealed in statistics on karate participants. For example, roughly 60 percent of the estimated four million Americans that practiced karate or taekwondo in 1993 were under 19 years of age. In addition, 40 percent of the increase in karate instruction between 1990 and 1995 has come from the pre-teen market (Ferguson, 1995: 138; Karate Kids, 1993: 15).

The larger the facility, the more adult students can also be attracted to enroll through offers of open training. For example, the contract allows the student to come in any time the dojo is open. Prospective adult students can take advantage of higher-priced private lessons during the day or classes during evening hours when children are in school, completing homework, or asleep. Rapid promotion of adults through the ranks also creates a pool of black-belt instructors that allows for greater class offerings, thereby completing the cycle.

Turnover considerations face all karate dojo; simply put, few students who begin training make it to the initial black-belt rank and beyond.[3] In this context, more traditional styles of karate training have become less viable from a business standpoint. Although containing many differences, traditional styles tend to emphasize discipline, training, contact sparring, philosophy, and a four-to-six-year timetable before reaching black-belt level. These characteristics contribute to a relatively high turnover rate. A business-oriented school can take this traditional approach and the risk of high turnover only if students are locked into contracts that require them to meet their financial obligations even if their interest in training has waned.

A more viable approach from a business standpoint is to repackage the art. Repackaging would include softening and sportifying karate to make it fun, while also offering belt packages and specials that promise regular advancement and promotions.[4] Such repackaging has become increasingly pervasive in the

U.S. karate instruction. A recent *Money* magazine analysis of popular karate programs notes that "a motivated student attending two classes a week could earn a black belt in three to four years at a cost of $1,500 to $2,000" (Karate Kids, 1993: 15).

To maintain enrollments in such packages, instructors must also discourage their students from exploring other styles and dojo. Exploration can lead to students questioning the nature and effectiveness of their instructor as well as the style of karate they have chosen. Exploration can also reveal differences in payment levels and practices and result in questions and protests by students and parents. Instructors tend to discourage exploration by either formal contractual provisions or informal sanction. The latter can include informing the student that the techniques being taught are too secret or dangerous to test or compare against other styles, questioning the students loyalty to the instructor or system, and temporarily suspending the student from the dojo.

As the arts become more sportified and oriented towards children, the tournament experience increases in importance. This experience consists primarily of kata competitions (empty-hand and weapons) and point sparring, as opposed to full-contact matches. Yet, tournaments face an inherent dilemma. Tournament promoters seek large numbers of participants and spectators. Size generates greater revenue from entry fees for spectators and participants and from sales of concessions (food and beverages), souvenirs (e.g., tee-shirts, patches), and rental space to martial arts equipment suppliers.[5] At the same time, however, parents and students seek a positive experience including reinforcement that they have chosen the best karate style, a desire shared by their karate instructors. This experience is more likely if the rules of the tournament are suited to their style of instruction rather than other styles—in effect, rules which can dissuade other competitors.

The inherent conflict between the numbers game and the risks of competition can be resolved in several ways. Two are increasingly prominent in the United States. The first option is to establish a large national karate association that holds closed tournaments for affiliated dojo. The second option is for a national association (or dojo) to hold an open tournament (all can attend) but require participants from other organizations and styles to follow the rules of the sponsoring association.

From a business standpoint, the ideal solution combines elements of these two options. The key is to establish large national karate associations or federations that offer a harmonized standard of competition, prestigious national ranking systems, and preferential treatment of competitors based on participation in affiliated tournaments. This approach is reflected in the activities of the North American Sport Karate Association (NASKA), whose circuit includes such prominent tournaments as the AKA Grand Nationals,

Battle of Atlanta, Compete Nationals, and Diamond Nationals. With large national tournaments drawing between 1,000-5,000 paying competitors and often twice as many spectators per event, the politics of inclusion and exclusion between karate associations and federations are increasingly played for high financial stakes (Corcoran 1994: 129-32; Compete at AAU, 1994: 23, 25; Battle of Atlanta, 1994: 10-11; Attend Compete, 1994: 14-15).

The emphasis on the commercial success of tournaments, however, also translates down to the level of instruction. In short, winning matters. Karate instructors try "to make a name for themselves by having a lot of students win tournaments and trophies, which draws more students into their school and makes them look good" (Johnson, 1994: 15). What does it take to win? In kata competitions, students need to demonstrate flashy techniques, such a high multiple kicks, gymnastic capabilities including cartwheels and backflips, and more recently the ability to perform with musical accompaniment. Students performing kata in tournament competitions tend to demonstrate little in the way of understanding the application (*bunkai*) of the techniques they are performing. The success rate for students performing more traditional kata in this context tends to be poor, often leading to the development of "modified" versions. In effect, image has become more important than the extent to which the techniques demonstrated make sense as martial arts.

For success in tournament sparring, students need to learn speed and how to score points. Clean, precise techniques that would be applicable in an actual defense situation matter less in most tournaments than speed, acting skills, and striking close enough to a target area with hand and foot for the judges to call a point. Whereas early tournaments in the United States largely relied on the control and skills of the participants to prevent injury, recent practice has relied on the extensive use of safety equipment and the easing of the requirement that competitors must make physical contact with the target area to score. The latter practice of noncontact (including to the body) has become increasingly common. Although popular among parents and students, because it eases the physical risk of competition, the practice contributes to the misleading sense of security that students have in their karate skills. In short, scoring points becomes the key to winning. Respect, discipline, true competence, and self-enlightenment do not (Theodoracopulos, 1992: 72-74).

The result is that tournaments often bring out the worst rather than the best in karate practitioners, instructors, and students alike. Competitors show disrespect to each other and to judges, at levels that can lead to parental shouting matches, instructors interfering in calls, and fights occurring between schools outside of the ring (Brawl Breaks Out, 1994: 11, 20-23). Black belts who serve as judges at times match up competitors based on political considerations of competing schools, make calls based on personal biases, or let the vocal complaints of parents and instructors sway their decisions. Students and instructors may bring home trophies, but the price to the arts is too high.

Rediscovering the Path

To what extent can the paradox between the goals set out by the martial ways and the growing reality of karate instruction and practice in the United States be resolved? As noted by Ochiai Hidy, the problem is not one of nationality. "Japanese students behave just like American students," Ochiai states. "Good students are good in any country and bad students are bad in any country" (Hidy, 1995: 15). My own experiences as a student in American and Japanese karate dojo reenforce Ochiai's observations. In both countries, I have seen students differ in the internal discipline they bring to the development of physical skills and conditioning. In both countries, I have seen students who differ in their loyalty, integrity, commitment, and willingness to let go of ego.

The problem instead lies with the way in which the arts are taught and the examples set for students by their instructors (Friman and Polland, 1994: 46-51). Here again, nationality is not the issue. Although shaped by the slightly different considerations of numbers and profit, demonstrations of rampantego, politics, and battles over turf can be found among high-ranking karate practitioners in Japan and the United States.

As noted by Yamaguchi Gosei, "karate is constantly in flux. Change brought on by separate people, places, and time is the art's most characteristic feature" (Yamaguchi, 1972: 6). Yet, through sportification, the budo aspects of karate are becoming lost. Reemphasizing these aspects will entail costs—in terms of influence, ego, and profit—for high-ranking karate practitioners. There are Japanese and American instructors who care little about numbers of students and who are selective in the students they allow to train in their dojo and in the time they spend with those students who demonstrate a desire and commitment to learn.

As noted by Peter Urban, "karatemen feel about their practice and style the way religious people feel about their religion" (Urban, 1967: 144). The comparison is an instructive one. Both religions and the martial arts often demand that practitioners blindly trust in the faith proffered by their leaders; meanwhile, the leaders focus on organization, numbers, and profits and offer little in the way of direction to their followers on the path to self-enlightenment. Thus, the first step towards positive change in karate instruction in the United States will be for more leaders to "restrain their egos" by recognizing their limitations and personal biases, and return to what Musashi Miyamoto referred to years ago as the "1,000 mile road of learning and enlightenment" (Urban, 1967: 145; Yamaguchi, 1972: 5-6; Musashi, 1974).

Notes

1. See the extensive coverage on this issue in *The New York Times* starting with the October 4, 1961, issue. On the growing importance of television revenues during this period (in the case of NCAA basketball), see Ken Rappaport, *The Classic*, p. 232.
2. These observations are based on the author's discussions with AAU representatives and negotiation observers.
3. For example, Oyama notes that less than ten percent make it to the rank of second-degree black-belt. Cited in Donohue, *Warrior Dreams*, p. 125.
4. Ferguson ("Let's Talk to the Master") notes that karate instruction has tended to "downplay the rough and tumble of the arts."
5. Century Martial Arts Supplies, for example, grosses $40 million annually in equipment sales (Ferguson, "Let's Talk to the Master," p. 142).

References

Battle of Atlanta draws 2,5000 competitors. (1994, September). *Black Belt*.
Brawl breaks out at Parker's internationals. (1994, December). *Black Belt*.
Corcoran, J. (1994). *The martial arts sourcebook*. New York: HarperCollins.
Donohue, J. (1994). *Warrior dreams: The martial arts and the American imagination*. Westport, CT: Bergin and Garvey.
Draeger, D., and Smith, R. (1980). *Comprehensive Asian fighting arts*. Tokyo: Kodansha International.
Draeger, D. (1974). *Modern bujutsu and budo*. Tokyo: Weatherhill.
Ferguson, T. (1995, October 23). Let's talk to the master, *Forbes*, pp. 138-42.
Friman, H., and Polland, R. (1994). Striving for realism: Concerns common to martial arts and law enforcement training. *Journal of Asian Martial Arts*, 3 (4): 46-51.
Funakoshi, G. (1981). *Karate-do: My way of life*. Tokyo: Kodansha International.
Funakoshi, G. (1988). *Karate-do nyumon*. Tokyo: Kodansha International.
Gluck, J. (1962). *Zen combat: A complete guide to Japanese martial arts*. New York: Ballentine Books.
Haines, B. (1968). *Karate's history and traditions*. Rutland, VT: Charles E. Tuttle.
Johnson, P. (1994, March). The real karate kid, *Black Belt*, p. 15.
Karate kids. (1993, September). *Money*.
Musashi, M. (1974). *A book of five rings* (Harris, V., Trans.). Woodstock, NY: Overlook Press.

Rapport, K. (1979). *The classic*. Kansas City: NCAA.

Skidmore, M. (1991, Summer). Oriental contributions to western popular culture: The martial arts. *Journal of Popular Culture 25* (1): 129-48.

Stepan, C. (1996, January). Redefining tae kwon do, *Tae Kwon Do Times*, pp. 50-58.

Theodoracopulos, T. (1992, August 21). Oriental ecstacy. *National Review 44* (17): 72-74.

Three thousand compete at AAU championships. (1994, December). *Black Belt*.

Two thousand two hundred attend compete nationals. (1994, July). *Black Belt*.

Urban, P. (1967). *The karate dojo: Traditions and tales of a martial art*. Rutland, VT: Charles E. Tuttle.

USAKF denied bid to regain governing status. (1994, October). *Black Belt*.

U.S. karate inc. adds key members. (1995, April). *Black Belt*.

A way to stop the spear. (1993, May 15). *The Economist*.

Yamaguchi, G. (1972). *The fundamentals of goju-ryu karate*. Los Angeles: Ohara Publications.

chapter 2

Martial Arts Marketing:
Putting the Customer First

by Yong Jae Ko, Ph.D.

Introduction

Interest and participation in the martial arts over the last twenty years has been tremendous. This growth has resulted in the awareness in many communities of the benefits of martial arts training. Along with rapid growth, increased competition has also emerged in this industry. Therefore, long-term viability and financial success of any martial arts school or program is contingent upon a better understanding of modern management principles, including the implementation of an effective marketing strategy (Ko, 2002). An effective marketing strategy will not only increase the level of customer satisfaction but will also be fundamental to the long-term financial success of any organization. Interest in modern management techniques, including the implementation of an effective marketing strategy, however, is relatively new to the martial arts community. Thus, efforts aimed at educating the martial arts industry as to the value of modern management practices and techniques are fundamental to the industry's ongoing success. One key aspect of modern management practices and techniques is the development of an effective marketing strategy. Consequently, this chapter explores the value of one of the most dominant marketing strategies, relationship marketing, as it applies to the martial arts industry.

The next section briefly reviews the evolution of martial arts as an emerging, global consumer products industry. This is followed by an examination of how relationship marketing can be applied to a martial arts organization. The chapter concludes by briefly suggesting opportunities for future research and practice.

Olympic Sports

judo, taekwondo, wushu???

Martial Arts as Global Consumer Product

There has been a phenomenal growth in the martial arts industry. Today, the globalization of Asian martial arts—through popular movies and a broader acceptance as a sport—has resulted in broader participation at the recreational, amateur, and professional levels. This growth has led to an increased awareness of and interest in martial arts throughout the world at all levels.

The growth of martial arts was due not only to the increased interest level among martial arts participants, but also to progressive efforts of leaders within the industry. For example, the modernization of instructional curriculum and the sportification of martial arts (i.e., martial arts as an Olympic sport) have accounted for some of the growth in the number of participants in such programs. In addition, the transition from a traditional fighting art to a competition-orientated sport, with the inclusion of martial arts programs in educational systems, has also been hypothesized to be a major catalyst behind the growth and popularity of many modern martial arts styles (Yang, 1997).

Martial arts globalization can be best illustrated in the case of taekwondo. Following judo, in 1994, taekwondo was selected to become an official Olympic event in the 2000 Games. Currently, the World Taekwondo Federation (WTF) is one of the largest martial arts organizations, representing more than 40 million members around the world and in more than 140 countries (Kim, 1994). The addition of taekwondo to the Olympics is evidence that taekwondo has developed into a global sport. As a result, these factors have pushed the participation level in taekwondo to over 2.5 million practitioners in the US alone (USTU, 1996).

In the United States, recent forecasts have estimated that the number of martial arts practitioners has increased 60 percent during the late 1990's, from nine million to more than 15 million people (Orlando, 1997). By industry counts, "enrollment in studios specializing in Eastern martial arts pursuits such as Karate and Taekwondo has about doubled over the last five years.... In the U.S. commercialized instruction now may be a $1.5 billion business ... (and) it was second only to computer networking services in its 1994 growth rate" (Ferguson, 1995: 138). It is estimated that roughly 1 out of 10 Americans at some time registered for martial arts lessons (Cox, 1993; cited by Yang, 1996). Clearly, martial arts have become a mainstream activity in not only Eastern cultures, but also in Western.

Currently, specific market segments of martial arts include: (a) classes offered by private martial arts schools and public health/fitness programs (e.g., YMCA/YWCA), (b) martial arts programs in higher education institutions, (c) local, regional, national, and international martial arts events, and (d) supporting organizations. Today, there are approximately 13,600 martial arts schools within the US (Reference USA, 1999).

Ko (1999) identified several factors that directly influenced the growth of the martial arts industry. They are:

- The change of lifestyle in the society (i.e., health and fitness consciousness)
- Women's participation in martial arts
- Enhancement of cultural diversity within a local community
- Increased number of violent crimes and public awareness of the importance of safety
- Increased demands for alternative types of education
- Emerging new programs and products
- Adaptation to a new management philosophy and marketing techniques
- Sportification and globalization of martial arts (e.g., taekwondo as a new Olympic event)
- Increases in the number of publications and public information resources
- Increase to media exposure

An increase in the number of participants has also resulted in a rapid increase in the number of martial arts schools and programs. As a result, this industry is becoming highly competitive. Consequently, school owners and martial arts organizations' leaders are actively beginning to employ modern management techniques, including marketing strategies. At the same time, a paradigm shift occurred in many martial arts organizations. As the number of practitioners increased, many martial arts organizations have become more formalized and institutionalized. For example, the United States Taekwondo

Union (USTU), the national governing body for taekwondo, developed specific regulations and policies to resolve current issues and prevent potential problems. For example, the USTU governs all local, regional, and national competitions and sets promotion standards to more effectively integrate this industry and to better align standards in the United States with the global taekwondo community. As a result, the USTU also developed formal structures for communication so that students, instructors, and referees have a single clearinghouse for all relevant information (Ko, 2002). This formalization of standards and procedures is a clear indication of the industry's maturation.

Although the current trend of growth and maturation in the martial arts industry is generating new opportunities for martial arts leaders, it is also creating numerous challenges as well. As local markets become more saturated with substitute offerings, the success of any single martial arts organization may depend on the degree to which the organization can satisfy its customers with quality service. To meet the diverse and sophisticated needs of an increasingly better-educated consumer, service quality will become the major competitive advantage for most successful martial arts organizations. A requirement in providing better service quality is to better understand the customer. In the next section, we examine one key technique for gaining this understanding: the use of relationship marketing.

sidebar 1
Martial Art Publications

Aikido Today	Karate Bushido
Arte d'Oriente	Karate Budo Journal
Black Belt	Kungfu Magazine
Bugeisha	Martial Arts Combat Sports
Classical Fighting Arts	Martial Arts Professional
Filipino Martial Arts	RAPID Journal
Furyu	Samurai
Inside Kung Fu	Tai Chi / Alternative Health
International Karate	Taijiquan Journal
Journal of Asian Martial Arts	Tai Chi Magazine
Journal of Japanese Sword Arts	Tae Kwon Do Times

sidebar 2
Martial Art Schools

Aikido	Mixed-Martial Arts
Arnis	Sambo
Baqua	Shaolin
Hapkido	Silat
Iaido	Sumo
Jiu Jitsu	Taekwondo
Judo	Taiji
Karate	Tangsudo
Kendo	Wing Chun
Kung-fu	Xingyi
Kuntao	Wushu

Relationship Marketing and the Martial Arts Business
Marketing is defined as:

> The process of planning and executing the conception, pricing, promotion, and distribution of ideas, goods, and services to create exchanges that satisfy individual and organizational objectives.
> – *Marketing News*, 1985

In the basic concept of marketing, the importance of customer orientation is highlighted. A customer orientation toward marketing holds that success will come to an organization that best determines the perceptions, needs, and wants of target markets and satisfies them through the design, communication, pricing, and delivery of appropriate and competitively viable offerings (Kotler and Andreasen, 1991). The marketing mindset of "customer-centeredness" requires that the organization systematically study the customers' needs, wants, perceptions, preferences, and satisfaction. Thus, marketing planning should begin with the consumer, not with the organization.

In the past, aggressive marketing efforts in martial arts lagged behind other industries and the rapid growth rate of the industry during the 1990's. Since then, several martial artists have developed business seminars to better educate school operators on modern business practices and techniques. These seminars focus on providing martial art school operators with valuable knowledge and techniques for the effective management and operation of a school (e.g., promotional strategy, membership contracts, billing methods, etc.) (Yang, 1997).

Additionally, a number of consulting companies have also emerged to improve the management of martial arts businesses, including:

- National Association of Professional Martial Artists (NAPMA)
- International Martial Arts Management Systems (IMAMS)
- Martial Arts Management Institute of Korea
- Martial Arts Marketers Association
- Global Financial
- American Management Services
- Triad Enterprises
- Korea Taekwondo Consulting Co.
- KICK
- Educational Funding Company (EFC), and,
- Karate International.

These organizations have not only provided new services and products to martial arts schools, but have also created additional market demand within the industry through better management practices. Consequently, many martial arts community leaders now realize that it is necessary to adopt modern management philosophies and to implement effective marketing strategies to remain competitive in a constantly changing and highly competitive market environment. Accordingly, the number of management and consulting companies has increased to meet the market demand. It appears that the demand for marketing and management services will continue to grow as long as the martial arts industry continues to experience growth and viability.

Nevertheless, and unfortunately, marketing philosophy and ethical practices have not always been a major focus in the industry. Some marketing practices have focused on short-term financial benefits rather than on the long-term success and the community well-being. The evolution of other highly competitive, consumer-oriented industries, however, can help to guide the martial arts industry. History has shown that a long-term, customer centered focus is at least one viable approach to realizing long-term success.

One approach to customer-oriented marketing, and the focus of this discussion, is called "relationship marketing." Hunt and Morgan (1994: 22) define relationship marketing as "all marketing activities directed toward establishing, developing, and maintaining successful relational exchange." In this relational exchange, interdependence is viewed as a central feature, and its role is to promote long-term relationships and mitigate short-term self-interest (Copulski and Wolf, 1991; Davis, 1995; Shani, 1997). In sum, three relationship marketing features are:

- emphasis on long-term relationship between customers and an organization (continuity),
- customizing marketing mix (i.e., product, promotion, price, and place) (individualization), and
- build customer loyalty and commitment (personal relationship). Relationship marketing has been seen as a positive force, enacted for the good of both customers and an organization.

The basic tenet of customer-centered organization and relationship marketing may provide a new paradigm of management philosophy and implications to martial arts organizations. Although the discussion of relationship marketing is a popular theme in other sport industry sectors, it is a relatively new concept within the martial arts industry. Regardless of its size and type (i.e., profit or non-profit, private and public), martial arts organizations should adapt the key concepts by recognizing and appropriately responding to the current customers' needs.

The success of developing and maintaining a positive relationship between martial arts organizations and their members depends on the degree to which we recognize and appropriately respond to customers' needs. In addition, relationship marketing suggests that martial arts organizations may be able to satisfy their customers not only by meeting the consumers' needs through quality services, but also by motivating them to actively participate in service production and consumption as a partner. The concept can be expanded to the development of relationship between martial arts organizations and the broader community (e.g., community relation, volunteerism, etc.), resulting in not only a viable business and employer, but also a better quality of life for all in the community.

In sum, the development of a positive long-term relationship with each customer is argued to be a fundamental factor in the long-term success of any martial arts organization. The implementation of a customer-centric, relationship marketing philosophy requires long-term commitment of leaders within martial arts organizations and each local business unit.

Conclusion and Future Opportunities

This discussion presents a big challenge to martial arts leaders in the 21st century. It also presents a big opportunity. As noted earlier, the practical

> Leaders should monitor their marketing practices using the highest ethical standards.

application of marketing concepts and strategies into the martial arts industry requires a collective and sustained effort among leaders. For the future development of the industry, leaders need to solve several problems.

First, business and marketing concepts, like relationship marketing, must be shared among martial arts leaders. Too often, martial arts leaders view customers as simply "students" whose main role is to respect tradition and be loyal to the instructor and school system. This results in a gap between martial arts tradition and relationship marketing philosophy, which is dominant in the West. As Kotler and Andreasen (1991) noted, martial arts industry leaders should make every effort to sense, serve, and satisfy the needs and wants of their customers and local communities. An effective marketing strategy can be designed based on the broader perspectives of martial arts service and its customers. In addition, martial arts need to be understood as a dynamically changing entity. Martial arts practitioners dynamically conceptualize their training based upon their cultural environment (Yang, 1996). Therefore, industry leaders need to assess market demand and monitor a constantly changing business environment, much like they monitor the evolution and changes within their art. For example, demographic shift (i.e., aging of baby boomers) in today's society requires that martial arts organizations develop new curriculum based on their customers' changing needs.

Second, there has been little research examining marketing in martial arts industry. To date, martial arts researchers have focused on such limited areas as philosophical, historical, cultural, and technical aspects. Many martial arts consulting companies limit their service to the tuition-collection function, often failing or unable to provide effective marketing strategies due to a lack of understanding or sophistication. Thus, research areas of marketing and management should be given special attention in this industry. For example, basic marketing strategies (e.g., price, products, promotional strategy, and distribution), service quality, and consumer behavior (i.e., psychological approaches of consumer's buying behavior) need to be explored in the martial arts industry.

Last, martial artists need to be ethically matured. Leaders should monitor their marketing practices using the highest ethical standards. When an industry has a sales orientation rather than a service orientation, the potential arises for customer abuse. In fact, most martial arts schools do not have a clearly articulated management philosophy or mission. Therefore, leaders should develop their management philosophy based at least in part on a marketing orientation where customer satisfaction and human development are highlighted. These efforts may redirect the future of martial arts so that the quality of each consumer's experience is optimized. Clearly, many opportunities and challenges remain.

Bibliography

Copulski, R. and Wolf, J. (1991, July/August). Relationship marketing: Positioning for the future. *Journal of Business Strategy*, 3, 16-26.

Cox, J. (1993). Traditional Asian martial arts training: A review. *Quest*, 45, 366-388.

Davis, J. (1995, Fall). Dependency, self-interest, and relationship marketing: A view of the nature of exchange. *Journal of Marketing*, 3, 17-23.

Ferguson, T. (1995, October 23). Let's talk to the master. *Forbes*, 156 (10): 138-142.

Hunt, S. and Morgan, R. (1994). Relationship marketing in the era of network competition. *Marketing Management*, 3(1), 18-28.

Kim, U. (1994). *Taekwondo*. Seoul, Korea: World Taekwondo Federation.

Ko, Y. (1999, March). *Martial arts industry in the new millennium*. Paper presented at the 1999 Annual Academic Symposium entitled "The Martial Arts for the Next Millennium" at the University of California, Berkeley.

San Francisco, CA.
Ko, Y. (2002). Martial arts industry in the new millennium. *Journal of Martial Arts Studies, 5,* 10-23.
Kotler, P. and Andreasen, A. (1991). *Strategic marketing for nonprofit organizations.* Englewood Cliffs, NJ: Prentice-Hall.
Marketing News (1985, March 1). AMA board approves new marketing definition. *Marketing News, 1.*
Reference USA (1999). http://reference.infousa.com/cgi-bin.
Shani, D. (1997). A framework for implementing relationship marketing in the sport industry. *Sport Marketing Quarterly, 11(2),* 9-15.
USTU (1996). *School/club handbook.* Colorado Springs, Colorado.
Yang, J. (1996). *American conceptualization of Asian martial arts: An interpretive analysis of the narrative of Taekwondo participants.* Unpublished doctoral dissertation, The University of North Carolina, Greensboro.
Yang, J. (1997). *Analyzing developmental process of American martial art school and introduction process of management system.* Unpublished manuscript.

chapter 3

The Globalization of Martial Arts: The Change of Rules for New Markets

by Yong Jae Ko, Ph.D. and Jin Bang Yang, Ph.D.

Illustration courtesy of www.iStock.com

Introduction

Historically, the martial arts have long been an important form of physical activity and education in East Asian countries (Ko, 2002). The martial arts industry has experienced tremendous growth and its recent growth has led to an increased awareness of and an involvement in martial arts around the world (Ko, 2002, 2003). As a result, the martial arts have become an integral part of sports and physical activity that convey a healthy lifestyle and cultural values with both an educational and entertainment function in many Western countries. The increased number of martial arts products, practitioners, organizations, and events reflects that martial arts have become an integral part of our society.

Today, the martial arts industry is rapidly evolving into a mature and highly competitive marketplace (Ko, 2002, 2003). In the U.S., for example, recent forecasts have estimated that the number of martial arts participants has increased 60 percent during the past decade, from 3.6 million people in 1993 to 6 million people in 2001 (NSGA, 2002). The number of commercial martial arts schools has also increased from 13,600 in 1999 to 14,500 in 2003 (InfoUSA, 2003). Meanwhile, the martial arts industry faces many challenges to compete with the major industries of both traditional and emerging sports and leisure activities.

As the martial arts continue to cross national borders and grow as a part of popular culture in the global community, martial arts literature has called for broader research on the globalization process and strategies applied by martial arts organizations. In reality, although the martial arts have been moving to greatly increase the range of choices available to consumers in different countries, adoption patterns have not always been responsive in ensuring the successful diffusion of the martial arts' educational and entertainment potential. For the martial arts to survive in this highly competitive environment, it is essential to develop a better understanding of the factors that influence the globalization of martial arts as a cultural product and the decision-making processes of martial arts consumers in various regions. The academic effort aimed at understanding these issues is essential not only for maintaining current success but also to fostering the industry's future growth. To date, however, the literature has neglected the diffusion process of Asian martial arts to Western society. Thus, there is very little known about the martial arts as global consumer products and limited scholarly efforts have been made to examine the issues.

Consequently, the purpose of this study is to examine the martial arts as a popular cultural product and to propose future research and examine the managerial implications for martial arts organizations. Specifically, this study furthers the exploration of the martial arts industry by examining its globalization process and its potential problems. In addition, there is a discussion of key strategies for the martial arts' further development in the global market and a set of obligations for the martial arts community leaders. This study may provide martial arts leaders with important managerial implications for developing effective management strategies targeted at martial arts practitioners in the global market. As of yet, there has not been any substantial research on this issue. This study will make both scientific and practical contributions.

GLOBALIZATION OF MARTIAL ARTS

Globalization is "the managerial process of integrating worldwide activities into a single world strategy by managing a network of differentiated but integrated subsidiaries, affiliates, alliances, and associations" (Tallman and Fladmoe-Lindquist, 2002: 124). While internationalization (i.e., international expansion/diversification) refers to a strategy of greater presence in international locations, globalization (i.e., global integration) involves a strategy of consolidating international markets and operations into a single worldwide strategic entity. Globalization is a strategic effort to treat the world as a single market, which requires various combinations of capabilities, strategies and resources (Tallman and Fladmoe-Lindquist, 2002).

The globalization of Asian martial arts through a broader acceptance as a global sport has resulted in an increased awareness of martial arts and broader participation at the recreational, amateur, and professional levels throughout the world (Ko, 2003). In particular, this transition from a traditional fighting art to a competition-orientated sport has been hypothesized to be a major catalyst behind the growth and popularity of many modern martial arts styles (Yang, 1997).

The Diffusion of Asian Martial Arts in the United States

From the mid-1880's to the early 1990's, Asian martial arts activities were practiced in limited areas of the United States. From 1884, Chinese laborers flocked to California mining towns and railroad construction sites, and Japanese immigrants moved to farmland in California and Hawai'i. These Asian immigrants practiced their own traditional martial arts within their communities (Corcoran and Farkas, 1983; Davey, 1996).

In 1902 and 1903, Japanese judo professional Yamashita Yoshiaki and Tomita Shumeshiro visited the United States, and formally introduced judo into American society (Corcoran and Farkas, 1983). However, it was not until after World War II that America had any significant exposure to Asian martial arts. When American troops occupied Japan, Korea, Okinawa, and some parts of China, many GIs had the chance to learn Asian martial arts, and to bring these arts back home. In some cases, they invited their foreign instructors to come to the United States to teach (USTU, 1990). According to Min (1996: 4), "the modern version of Taekwondo owes its character to those masters who joined together after Korea's liberation from colonial rule (of Japan) to establish a Korean martial art that would be able to transcend national borders and allow Korea to share some of its fine traditions with the rest of the world."

In the 1950's, there were several historical events that promoted Japanese karate and Korean taekwondo to the American public. In 1952, a Korean-Japanese, Mas Oyama toured the United States to introduce karate to the American public; in 1953, ten prominent Japanese martial arts instructors' demo tours followed (Yang, 1996). Table 1 presents a brief chronology of the early diffusion of Asian martial arts to the United States. Martial arts enjoyed an increase in popularity following the release of Bruce Lee's movie, "Enter the Dragon" in 1973, following the television series "Kung Fu" in 1972. Since then, Asian martial arts have become a favorite theme in Hollywood movies and television shows (Donohue, 1994; Graper, 1983). "The Karate Kid" (1984), "Best of the Best" (1989), and "Crouching Tiger, Hidden Dragon" (2000) are only a few examples of such media.

With the popularity gained through the early diffusion of martial arts around the world, in the 1970's, Asian martial arts in the United States underwent significant changes that gave momentum to their popularization. One change was that American students achieved instructor status. Another milestone was the end of the Vietnam War, an important event for the international diffusion of taekwondo. With the Korean army as a Western ally, a taekwondo instructor unit was dispatched primarily to teach particular U.S. military forces and civilians, but also resulted in spreading the art to other American soldiers. After the war, soldiers who learned the art, and more significantly their Korean instructors, moved to the United States, accelerating the diffusion of taekwondo, which, at the time, was considered only a minor art.

The Current Status of Three Major Asian Martial Arts

The globalization of martial arts can best be illustrated in the cases of judo, taekwondo, and wushu/gongfu. Developed by Dr. Kano Jigoro in the 1880's, judo spread all over the world as a result of Japanese emigration. Judo was the first martial art to become an Olympic sport at the 1964 Tokyo, Japan, games. Today, the International Judo Federation (IJF) lists about 180 members and over eight million practitioners in the world (International Judo Federation, 2007). The Japanese Government has institutionalized cultural education with the official "cultural visa," which allows visitors a longer stay in Japan for cultural studies (Goldstein-Gidoni, 2005), which include judo and the other martial arts. The Japanese Government has also used the martial arts as an avenue for the promotion of Japanese culture abroad.

In South Korea, although various forms of martial arts have existed, Korean martial arts leaders chose taekwondo as the definitive Korean martial art in an attempt to promote its development internationally (IOC, 2007). As a result, the World Taekwondo Federation (WTF) was formed in 1973 as the legitimate governing body of the sport. The organization is made up of taekwondo national governing bodies. Currently, the WTF has become one of the largest martial arts organizations in the world, representing members in 185 countries (WTF, 2007). The increased popularity of taekwondo and its addition to the Olympics in 2000 clearly indicates that taekwondo has become a global sport. However, behind the development of modern taekwondo is the strong support of the Korean Government. As part of reaffirming cultural identity, the propagation of taekwondo around the world was conceived as an important government goal. Today, government leaders emphasize promoting Korean culture overseas to develop diplomatic relationships under the movement of globalization (*segyehwa*), and taekwondo is perceived to be one avenue for this international development (Kim, 1996). A recent government plan to build a mega facility (Taekwondo Park) is perceived to be a catalyst for this movement.

While the Japanese and Koreans have already set an international standard for judo and taekwondo, respectively, Chinese martial arts (e.g., *wushu*) are under severe pressure to accommodate the demands of modernization and cultural globalization (Henning, 2006). Although wushu is not yet accepted as an Olympic sport, the International Wushu Federation continues to grow as a world governing body, with 86 member associations in five continents in 2001. The growth of Chinese martial arts around the world can also expose more people to diverse forms of physical activity (*People's Daily*, 2001).

There have been many historical events that played major roles for the martial arts' globalization. Although each martial arts discipline has its unique developmental process from different historical backgrounds, there are several common factors that influence the globalization process. They include but are not limited to:

(1) the transformation of values of martial arts training (Donohue, 1994; Ko, 2002),
(2) modernization of the instructional curriculum (Yang, 1997),
(3) promotional efforts made by governments of the martial arts countries-of-origin and increased marketing efforts in the martial arts business (Ko, 2003),
(4) global expansion of martial arts through sportification and formalization (Ko, 2002; Yang, 1997), and
(5) the diversification of martial arts products such as movies (e.g., "Karate Kids" and "Last Samurai"), fitness programs (e.g., Billy Blanks' Taebo), and the emergence of a new genre of martial arts events (e.g., mixed martial arts competitions).

Illustrations courtesy of www.iStock.com

As observed in the cases of judo, taekwondo, and wushu, the modern history of the martial arts shows that the martial arts as global cultural products have been formalized and institutionalized through sportification (Ko, 2002). The multinational organizations (e.g., IJF and WTF) have developed organizational structures, policies, and procedures to enhance the effectiveness and efficiency of administration and daily management. For example, the WTF was developed to be a global structure through which member organizations (i.e., national governing bodies) develop grass-root programs and elite competitors, who compete in various international events (e.g., Olympics, World Taekwondo Championship, and Universiad Games). For this purpose, the organization developed specific regulations and policies to resolve current issues and prevent potential problems on such issues as competitors, coaches, referees, sponsors, training programs, facilities, equipment, media, and daily management and administration procedures.

Martial art organizations, particularly the IJF and WTF, managed their international network with differentiated but integrated affiliates, alliances, and associations. International diversification and global integration allows martial arts organizations to generate additional revenues in multiple national markets by exploiting new assets and gaining new market power by increasing their size. On the other hand, the globalization process also creates several important issues that need to be resolved. Political and cultural value conflicts and market strategies are key issues, among many others.

Governance and Politics

As each of the martial arts organizations grows to be an international sport structure, often they are used as a function of government and as an instrument of national power and interest (Calhoun, 1987). As a result, political conflicts may exist between headquarters and member organizations that represent the needs of their local markets. This is true, particularly for the martial arts organizations in developmental stages. In this case, it is very important for martial arts organizations in a developmental stage to create an organizational structure supporting strong integration (centralization) among all affiliated members. In this process, however, they need to be capable of controlling this integration without losing the unique qualities and values of individual member organizations by ignoring their needs (Bartlett and Ghoshal, 1989). As martial arts organizations mature and grow, it is suggested that organizations should be able to decentralize operational responsibilities to differentiated subsidiaries. This process may dramatically reduce the "command and control" role of the headquarters in favor or "coordination and coaching." In this case, a martial arts organization's role in management and control needs to be oriented toward efficiency in "know-how logics" (Tallman and Fladmoe-Lindquist, 2002). Therefore, these types of changes in leadership style will results in a paradigm shift in the management and political environments of many martial arts organizations.

Tallman and Fladmoe-Lindquist (2002) outlined some positive consequences of the strategic configuration of multinational organizations: a) the capability to generate dynamic synergy, b) the ability to use alliances to explore new knowledge, rather than focus on whole ownership to protect old knowledge, and c) a favorable response from local markets toward products through empowerment. Central administration needs to develop skills at coordinating, not controlling, on a global basis. Thus, the administration becomes responsible for setting standards and building frameworks rather than actively managing operations on a daily basis. As a result, headquarters knows when to set standards (e.g., financial reporting) and when to stay out of transactions. Fairness, social justice, and effective distribution strategies must also be considered.

Culture

Culture still matters in the martial arts business. Culture is a set of socially acquired behavior patterns transmitted symbolically through language and other means to the members of a particular society, which distinguishes the members of one category of people from another (Wallendorf and Reilly, 1983). Understanding different and diverse cultures could enhance the organization's performance (e.g., revenue generation), because such understanding leads to more viable market penetration (Hilliard-Jones, 1996). However, the major problems faced by cross-cultural and international management stem from both the value differences and incongruency between the central administration's underlying core values and the values central to the host cultural setting (Lachman, Nedd, and Hinning, 1994; Penaloza and Gilly, 1999).

In consideration of the martial arts as a popular cultural product, one of the main goals of headquarters is to spread cultural values and technical knowledge of the martial arts among members throughout the world (Ko and Pastore, 1998). In the process of diffusion of cultural products, it is an undeniable reality that many members of affiliated organizations may face value conflicts between the culture of the local market and the country of origin. Thus, it is very important for martial arts leaders to understand that fundamental cultural differences may exist among countries and organizations. Additionally, these differences may conceivably influence organizational practices (Ko and Pastore, 1998). In this case, a main source of the value conflict may be the Confucian values of the Eastern mindset and the pragmatism of Western practitioners. According to Kim (1996: 33), "Confucianism sees all human relations in the light of a vertical relationship.... In an organization, it meant employees were to obey employers and juniors to respect seniors." In addition, collectivism and individualism (e.g., Hofstede, 1991) may explain some important cultural gaps among international members.

In collectivistic cultures, the self is construed in interdependent terms as a connected, relational entity that is expected to fit in by maintaining interpersonal relationships and group harmony. On the other hand, in individualistic cultures, the self is construed as an independent entity that is expected to stand out by becoming distinguished from others through personal accomplishment. For example, due to the difference of cultural values, dealing directly with conflict or problems in North America is generally considered appropriate while in Korea and other Far East cultures, the same behavior may be seen as impolite or overly aggressive (Tushman and O'Reilly, 1997). As another example, building a positive relationship is a prerequisite in doing business in many Asian countries with collectivistic cultures, while, in Western cultures, business relationships tend to be straightforward and dominated by overt legal and financial negotiations.

Therefore, leaders in martial arts organizations need to be aware of how cultural differences impact organizational performance in diverse international markets and how to manage cultural values and diversity issues within their organizations (Doney, Cannon, and Mullen, 1998). This will ultimately help enhance efficiency and effectiveness in their job performance. Although standardization and formalization (hardware) are very important in the globalization process, leaders should recognize unique cultural values (software) of local markets and help develop a third culture that represents neither the cultural values from country of origin nor the culture of local country, through diffusion of martial arts. In reality, while martial arts embody the cultural beliefs and values of the country of origin, through the assimilation process, their meaning is gradually altered for consistency with the local culture and identities of native participants (e.g., Duda and Allisaon, 1990). Thus, cultural training (e.g., human resource management) may improve understanding of cultural gaps and help incorporate unique local management styles and attract the best worldwide talent. Capable human resources are the most important asset to martial arts organizations and their growth.

Market Orientation and Trust

The long-term viability and financial success of the martial arts organizations are contingent upon a better understanding of consumers that involves identifying consumers' unique needs and satisfying them by providing quality services. This topic has historically been of little interest to this industry and so its application is relatively new (Ko, 2003; 2004).

Market orientation is the organization-wide generation of market intelligence and dissemination of that intelligence across affiliate organization members (Jaworski and Kohli, 1993; Kohli and Jaworski, 1990). Market orientation supports the management philosophy that highlights the central importance of customers. The lack of market orientation may result in demand uncertainty and critical management errors in the global market context. This situation emerges when, for example, organizations launch new products for which there is no latent demand, or when organizations fail to launch products that would have been successful, which represent latent demand for which there is no supply (Eliashberg, Lilien, and Rao, 1997). Therefore, martial arts organizations need to continue to focus on who their customers are, why they participate in martial arts and how to satisfy them. The market-oriented organizational culture and management philosophy will also help develop trust among members within an organization.

Martial arts participants seek to learn different cultures and philosophies embodied in the traditional values of martial arts (Ko & Valacich, 2004). This indicates that consumers perceive martial arts training as a cultural learning process. Through this process, they learn the traditional values of martial arts training (e.g., respect, perseverance, discipline, self-control, modesty, integrity, and loyalty) while they satisfy their own needs (e.g., physical, mental, and social benefits) (Boudreau, Folman, and Konzak, 1995; Kennedy, 1997; Ko and Valacich, 2004; Yang, 2000). However, more systematic research needs to be conducted for a better understanding of the global market and successful implementation of marketing strategies. This more systematic approach will ensure that this dual process of assimilating cultural values through physical activity remains as the major competitive advantage for martial arts organizations (Ko, 2003).

Illustration courtesy of www.iStock.com

Illustration courtesy of www.iStock.com

Discussion & Conclusions

The globalization of the martial arts will continue. As globalization causes dramatic changes in the business environment, forecasting such changes is crucial for the preparation of responses by the affected parties (Czinkota and Ronkainen, 2005). Thus, the future success of martial arts organizations is dependent upon how well they adapt to a continuously changing market environment.

The ultimate goal of martial arts organizations is to develop network structures to create new value through the integration of various kinds of knowledge, resources, and capabilities across its geographically dispersed national organizations. This process can be accomplished by respecting the cultural uniqueness of local market and the organization's transparency and accountability. Additionally, the central administration in the various headquarters will continue to be confronted with re-distribution issues in regard to revenue and power. To be a true global cultural product, the ownership of martial arts should be equally shared among the members. The martial arts are no longer the property of their countries of origin. In addition, to deem it a "global sport," martial arts leaders must focus not only on the number of member nations (breadth), but also on the number of people who participate in each nation (depth), particularly in countries that are politically and geographically isolated.

TABLE 1: A brief chronology of the diffusion of Asian martial arts to the United States*

Years	Style	Events
1848-1863	gongfu	Chinese laborers imported to California for the Gold Rush
Late 1880	Japanese	Japanese immigrants to Hawai'i and California practiced their traditional arts
1879	judo	United States President Grant visited and observed Jigoro Kano's demonstration
1889	judo	Kano demonstrated judo to visiting American dignitaries
1889	judo	Ladd, Yale University professor studied judo at the Kodokan
1902	judo	Yamashita Yoshiaki, as the first Japanese judo instructor to teach judo in the U.S.
1903	judo	Tomita Shumeshiro taught judo in Princeton and Columbia Universities
1907	judo	Ito Takugoro founded the first American judo school in Seattle, Washington
1921		The movie *Outside Women* showed Asian martial arts to the general audience
1930	wushu	Ark-Yuey Wong organized gongfu training group within Chinese community
1933	karate	Higaonna Kamesuke from Okinawa visited Hawai'i
1934	karate	Miyagi Chosun was invited to Hawai'i to teach karate
1936	kendo	Mori Torao immigrated to Los Angeles, CA, and begun to teach kendo
1940	judo	The first intercollegiate judo competition held in San Jose, California
1941	judo	Many Americans practiced judo in Japanese relocation camps
1946	karate	Robert Trias founded the first karate school in the U.S. mainland in Phoenix, Arizona
1949	judo	Judo was recognized as an official sport by AAU
1952	karate	Mas Oyama toured 32 states for demonstration of karate
1953	karate	Nishiyama Hidetaka & other Japanese prominent martial artists toured US military base
1955	karate	Ohshima Tsutomu began to teach karate in Los Angeles, CA; first time teaching orthodox Japanese style karate in the U.S.
1955	taekwondo	Atlee Chittim began to teach Taekwondo in Texas after he returned from Korea
1955	karate	Robert Trias organized the first karate tournament in Phoenix, Arizona
1956	taekwondo	Jhoon Rhee moved to Texas from Korea and taught taekwondo, becoming the father of American Taekwondo
1959	gongfu	Alan Lee began to teach Shaolin Gongfu in New York
1960	taekwondo	Henry Cho moved to New York to teach taekwondo; first in East Coast
1960	gongfu	Bruce Lee opened his first school in Seattle, WA
1964	hapkido	Choi Sea Oh introduced hapkido in Los Angeles, CA
1973	gongfu	Bruce Lee's movie *Enter the Dragon* became a milestone for the increased awareness of Asian martial arts

Directions for Future Research

Many questions remain. Once a basic understanding of the global expansion of martial arts and its diverse market is attained, more specific questions, like the following, should be explored: How can leaders enhance the efficiency and effectiveness of martial arts organizations? What are key strategies to promote martial arts products, services, and events? What changes should be made in marketing and management strategies? How do cultural diversity factors influence strategies for distribution of the martial arts in the global marketplace? What marketing and promotional strategies would be most effective in targeting specific target markets (subcultures)? To what degree are various subgroups within a specific member-nation satisfied and how do they develop loyalty, and how could marketing strategies impact such development? What are perceptions and attitudes that the general public developed toward martial arts, organizations and events? And, finally, what should be done to promote martial arts as true global products? Answering such questions would greatly assist in establishing a useful understanding of global consumers who participate in martial arts and provide the leaders in this industry with insights for the development of global market strategies.

References

Bartlett, C., and Ghoshal, S. (1989). *Managing across borders: The transnational solution.* Boston, MA: Harvard Business School Press.

Boudreau, F., Folman, R., and Konzak, B. (1995). Parental observations: Psychological and physical changes in school-age karate participants. *Journal of Asian Martial Arts, 4*(4), 51-69.

Calhoun, D. (1987). *Sport, culture, and personality.* Champaign, IL: Human Kinetics.

Corcoran, J. and, Farkas, E. (1983). *Martial arts: Tradition, history, and people.* New York: Galley Books.

Davey, H. (1996). Donn Draeger and International Hoplology Society. *Journal of Asian Martial Arts, 5*(1), 96-103.

Czinkota, M., and Ronkainen, I. (2005). A forecast of globalization, international business and trade: report from a Delphi study. *Journal of World Business, 40,* 111-123.

Donohue, J. (1994). *Warrior dreams: The martial arts and the American imagination.* Westport, CT: Bergin and Garvey.

Doney, P., Cannon, J., and Mullen, M. (1998). Understanding the influence of national culture on the development of trust. *Academy of Management Review, 23*(3), 601-620.

Duda, J., and Allison, M. (1990). Cross-cultural analysis in exercise and sport psychology: A void in the field. *Journal of Sport and Exercise Psychology, 12*, 114-131.

Edwards, H. (1979). *Sociology of sport.* Homewood, IL: Dorsey.

Eliashberg, J., Lilien, G., and Rao, V. (1997). Minimizing technological oversights: A marketing research perspective. In Carud, R., Nayyar, P., and Shapira, Z., (Eds.). *Technological innovation: Oversights and foresights.* New York: Cambridge University Press, 214-230.

Foster, A. (1986). The nature of the martial arts and their change in the west. In S. Kleinman (Ed.). *Mind and body: East meets west.* Champaign, IL: Human Kinetics.

Goldstein-Gidoni, O. (2005). The production and consumption of 'Japanese Culture' in the global cultural market. *Journal of Consumer Culture, 5*, 155-179.

Graper, D. (1983). The kung-fu movie genre: A functionalist perspective. In S. Thomas (Ed.). *Culture and communication: Methodology, behavior, artifacts, and institutions.* Critical Studies in Communication, V. 3. Norwood, NJ: Ablex. 153-158.

Henning, S. (2006). China's new wave of martial studies scholars. *Journal of Asian Martial Arts, 15*(2), 8-21.

Hilliard-Jones, A. (1996). Consumers of color are changing the American marketplace. *Marketing News, 30*(24), 8.

Hofstede, G. (1991). *Cultures and organizations: Software of the mind.* Berkshire, UK: McGraw-Hill Co.

Jaworski, B., and Kohli, A. (1993). Market orientation: Antecedents and consequences. *Journal of Marketing, 57* (July), 53-70.

International Judo Federation (n.d.). *The diffusion of Judo.* Retrieved August 31, 2007 from http://www.ijf.org/corner/qCornerView.asp?Page=1&MenuCode=DJ&Idx=48IJF.

International Olympic Committee (n.d.). *Taekwondo Olympic sport since 2000.* Retrieved August 31, 2007 from http://www.olympic.org/uk/sports/programme/index_uk.asp?SportCode=TK

Kim, E. (1996). *A cross-cultural reference of business practices in a New Korea.* Westport, CT: Quorum Books.

Ko, Y. (2002). Martial arts industry in the new millennium. *Journal of Martial Arts Studies, 5*, 10-23.

Ko, Y. (2003). Martial arts marketing: Putting the customer first. *Journal of Asian Martial Arts, 12*(2), 9-15.

Ko, Y., and Pastore, D. (1998). Analyzing cultural values within a sport organization: The case of the United States Taekwondo Union members. *The Journal of the International Council for Health, Physical Education, Sport, and Dance, 35*(1), 37-41.

Ko, Y., and Valacich, J. (2004). *Why people participate in martial arts: An analysis of motivation factors*. Paper presented at the Sport Marketing Association Conference. Memphis, Tennessee.

Kohli, A., and Jaworski, B. (1990). Market orientation: The construct, research propositions, and managerial implications. *Journal of Marketing, 54* (April), 1-18.

Lachman, R., Nedd, A., and Hinnings, B. (1994). Analyzing cross-national management and organizations: A theoretical framework. *Management Science, 40*(1), 40-55.

Min, K. (1996, Spring). Taekwondo philosophy in the Olympic movement. *USTU Taekwondo Journal,* 4-5.

National Sporting Goods Association (2002). *The super study of sports participation*. Fort Mill, SC: American Sports Data.

People's Daily (2001, December 29). Wushu seeks to become Olympic sport. Retrieved August 31, 2007 from http://www.china.org.cn/english/2001/Dec/ 24469.htm.

Roberts, J. (2000). Developing new rules for new markets. *Journal of Academy of Marketing Science, 28*(1), 31-44.

Tillman, S., and Fladmoe-Lindquist, K. (2002). Internationalization, globalization, and capability-based strategy. *California Management Review, 51*(1), 116-135.

Tushman, M. and O'Reilly III, C. (1997). *Winning through innovation: A practical guide to leading organizational change and renewal*. Boston, MA: Harvard Business School Press.

United States Taekwondo Union (1990). *Taekwondo instructor manual*. The United States Taekwondo Union.

Wallendorf, M., and Reilly, M. (1983). Ethnic migration, assimilation, and consumption. *Journal of Consumer Research, 10*(3), 292-302.

World Taekwondo Federation (n.d.). Retrieved August 31, 2007 from http://www.wtf.org/.

Yang, D. (2000). A new perspective of martial arts education for the 21st century. *Journal of Physical Education, Recreation, Sport, and Dance, 36*(3), 22-27

Yang, J. (1996). *American conceptualization of Asian martial arts: An interpretive analysis of the narrative of taekwondo participants*. Unpublished Doctoral Dissertation. The University of North Carolina at Greensboro.

Yang, J. (1997). *Analyzing developmental process of American martial arts school and introduction process of management system*. Unpublished manuscript.

chapter 4

Nihonto: A Legal Perspective on Japanese Swords and Their Intrinsic Value

by Andrew Tharp, B.S.

"The history of the sword is the history of humanity."

— Sir Richard F. Burton

Above scene is from the graphic novel series, *Tales of the Hermit*, by O. Ratti and A. Westbrook. © Futuro Designs and Publications.

The sword is a powerful symbol. For as long as civilization can remember, it has represented war, nobility, power, and justice. Yet all cultures have modified, enhanced, or fixed the sword to mold to their way of life. The symbol of the sword is ever prevalent, but always uniquely represented. Japan has always had a particular reverence for the sword. The *nihonto*, commonly called the samurai sword, has always been a source of pride for the Japanese people. This is not to say the European sword is any less important or potent, but that Western culture did not embrace the sword with the same fervor as the Japanese.

Nihonto hold a special position in Japanese history. They are not just weapons of war; they are artwork, pieces of jewelry, symbols of status, and representations of the "soul of the samurai" (Yumoto, 1997). There are traditional martial arts, theater, artwork, and etiquette centered entirely on the sword (Yumoto, 1997: 12). Japanese smiths sign each sword they make, and the swords are often given names by their owners (Ratti and Westbrook, 1991). Some swords used in World War II had been passed down from warrior generation to warrior generation for over six hundred years (Yumoto, 1997:

12). Those smiths who make the best swords each year have work that is forever enshrined as a national treasure. In fact, some swordsmiths have even attained the rank of "living national treasure" for their contributions to the arts (Agency, website). There is even a government organization that has the sole responsibility of the registration and preservation of the Japanese sword (Nihon Bujutsu, website). As a result of such reverence, to this day Japan has the most well-preserved swords in the world, both in quality and quantity.

Why is that the case? An intense analysis of both the culture of the Japanese sword as well as the legal systems that surround it will attempt to answer that question. First we will examine the culture that surrounds the sword and its history, and then we will look at three specific legal elements. The first is about the registration of swords, the second concerns the import and export of swords, and the third is centered on the manufacture of swords.

Japanese Sword History and Culture

The history of the Japanese sword could, and has, filled many books, but this section will attempt to distill the most important information. For the purposes of this chapter, the Japanese sword will refer only to *nihonto* (or Japanese-made swords, as opposed to Japanese styled swords, not made in Japan). Like many other aspects of Japanese culture, nihonto evolution demonstrates a decided cycle of massive change, followed by long periods of stagnancy. This can likely be traced back to both the lack of trade and a culture of isolation, which created a relatively unchanged and singular form of sword.

The most common form of the Japanese sword is a single-bladed sword of about thirty inches, designed for use with one or two hands (Yumoto, 1997: 24). Like the Western sword, the Japanese sword has undergone several reincarnations. As with many other aspects of Japanese culture, the sword was imported from China in its infancy (Yumoto, 1997: 23). The earliest Japanese swords were very similar to Chinese swords from the same period (generally anytime before CE 650). It was not until the Heian period (794 to 1191) that Japanese swords began to take on what is now their distinct form (Yumoto, 1997: 24). During this period the primary form of warfare was mounted (Yumoto, 1997: 24). The curvature of the sword was more suited to slashing from horseback than were the previous straight swords, used primarily for stabbing. The swords of this period are generally referred to as *tachi*, and were worn with the blade facing downward, much like the early modern cavalry saber (Ratti and Westbrook, 1991: 256).

Note: The term *nihonto* can include several different kinds of swords from Japan—while most people associate it with the longsword (*katana*), it can also be applied to the short sword (*wakizashi*), or the knife-sized sword (*tanto*).

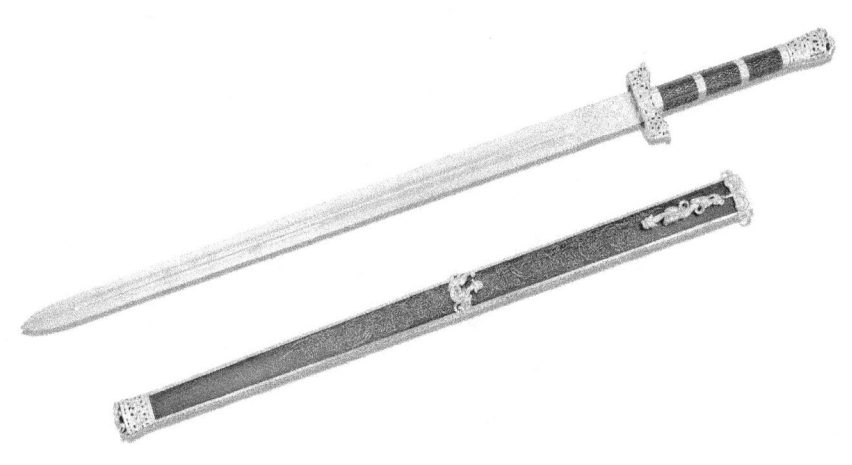

This sword is a recreation of what would have been common in the Han period of China (206 BCE–200 CE). It is would have been very similar to early period Japanese swords.

Later the sword evolved into what is now typically called the *katana* (Ratti and Westbrook, 1991: 256). The sword kept its characteristic curvature, but the need for mounted combat fell dramatically. At this point, the sword took on an entirely different place. It was shortened and worn blade up in the belt, rather than blade down. It was carried as a self-defense weapon by the samurai and was superseded as the primary weapon of war. The *naginata* (halberd) and *yumi* (bow and arrow) took its place (Yumoto, 1997: 24). The European sword also saw a similar evolution, but the katana continued to retain its curvature, whereas most self-defense swords in Europe relied on the point of the weapon (Oakeshott, 2007). Why nihonto retained their curved, cutting-focused structure is up for debate, but it probably has to do with both the manufacture of the weapons as well as the culture surrounding them.

When outlining the manufacture of a Japanese sword, it is important to note that there are many artisans who devote their entire lives in training to make each part of the sword. In this chapter we will focus on the forging of the blade, but there are also individuals who polish and sharpen swords, make the handle and guard (known as the "furniture"), and make the scabbard. A completed sword includes work by all of these artisans. It is also important to note at this point the seriousness with which a smith undertakes his work. Like most Japanese craftsmen, the swordsmith has a patron deity. Every forge has a deity shelf, where prayers are offered before, during, and after the creation of the sword. Swordsmiths believe they have divine assistance when creating their works (Yumoto, 1997: 99).

A wooden display stand for a tanto and it fittings.

There are generally considered to be four steps in forging a blade (Ratti and Westbrook, 1991: 259). The first is rough forging. This is when the traditional iron (*tamahagane*) is treated to create steel. The iron is heated and then folded, and the process is repeated twelve to fifteen times. This creates between 4,000 and 32,000 layers. This is also the process that creates the *hada*, or grain, within the blade. The heating and fold take the carbon that lies dormant in the charcoal and infuse it with the iron, creating steel. After the rough forging, the steel is shaped into the final form desired by the smith. The steel pieces are heated and fused together to make a billet of sword-shaped steel. Next is the clay covering and heating process. The blade is covered in a thin layer of clay, the composition of which is generally proprietary to the smith. The clay layer is generally thinner toward the blade (*ha*) and heavier toward the back (*mune*). Next, the clay-covered sword is heated in a kiln. The final step is the quenching of the blade. The heated blade is submerged, typically in saltwater, although, like the clay, many smiths use different mixtures. The clay makes the blade cool unevenly, creating both the curvature of the blade and the dividing line between the hard and soft sections of the blade (*hamon*). At this point, the completed blade is sent to the polisher for finishing (Yumoto, 1997: 98–109).

The forging of the sword is essential to its form, but so is the culture that surrounds it. The traditional martial arts of the Japanese sword are *kendo* and *iaido* (before the U.S. occupation in World War II, they were called *kenjutsu* and *iaijutsu*) (Ratti and Westbrook, 1991: 24). Like most traditional elements of Japanese culture, these arts are ritualistic and steeped in mysticism, but highly effective. Iaido is a key element to the form of the Japanese sword. The slightly curved blade with a long handle is the only acceptable shape that allows for the fluid motions of drawing and sheathing the blade that are the foundation of iaido (Suino, 2004). This fact shows one of the many cultural reasons the Japanese sword has remained in a similar state for over six hundred years. While it is probably impossible to argue the superiority of the Japanese systems of swordsmanship, it is evident that martial arts and other cultural norms have influenced the sword. Although it has certainly gone through some changes, what is most significant about the Japanese sword are the ways in which it has remained the same.

Tamahagane (a) must be purchased from the NBTHK. After heating in a furnace (b), two pieces of harder steel are being folded with a softer piece in the middle (c). This gives the final sword flexibility as well as hardness. It also allows the sword to both hold a razor sharp edge, but not snap when put under pressure.

The modern view of the weapon is significantly different from the historical perspective, but it is still essential to understanding why the nihonto has survived this long and is still being manufactured and preserved with traditional methods. In the West the sword died long ago. While weapons were still commonly issued in the American Civil War, most mortal wounds did not come from swords (Sayers, website). From the time of the American Civil War to World War I the sword almost entirely disappeared from the battlefield. This is mostly attributable to the invention of the repeating pistol as a sidearm (Britannica, website). The reduction in cavalry led to a near extinction of the sword on the battlefield. Today many militaries use swords as a uniform piece for formal occasions, but they have not been routinely used on the battlefield in more than a century (Britannica, website). This is not true in Japan, where even up until the end of World War II the Japanese military was still carrying and using swords.

Again, this derives from an intense need for constancy and strong traditionalism. The warrior caste (*bushi*) of Japan carried swords for most of its history. The sword was carried as a mark of nobility and station (Yumoto, 1997: 12). There were, again, strong traditions related to the wearing, removing, and carrying of the sword. Wearing the sword was an art in itself, with as much depth and importance as the art of actually using the blade. Whether or not the sword was actually an effective weapon on the modern battlefield was irrelevant. Members of the new warrior caste (military officers) not only desired but were expected to wear the weapons of their forefathers. In some cases, they were even wearing the physical weapons of their forefathers, as many swords had been passed down for generations and were simply refitted to modern military standards (Yumoto, 1997: 13).

Today the sword lives on in the popular culture of Japan. Many movies, anime, and books prominently feature the nihonto, and museums feature huge displays of antique blades (NBTHK, website). This is not so different from the West, where our popular culture also often centers on the sword, but there is a major difference. Collectors of Western swords are generally considered collectors of militaria or antiquity. Collectors of nihonto are considered art collectors. This may not seem like a major difference, but in effect, it creates a whole new dynamic to the market and preservation of the weapons. In general, nihonto are not only collected for their historical value, but also for their intrinsic beauty (Yumoto, 1997: 15). Today some modern smiths can still charge upwards of $10,000 for a modern-made blade with no military value. Nihonto are traded and auctioned as pieces of fine art and given the same valuations. Unlike Western swords, they are not traded based on what pattern or military used them, or what engagements they might have been involved in, but rather on what swordsmith (artist) made them, as well as the quality of the hada and hamon. Today a quality nihonto is incredibly expensive and takes an expert to determine its value (Yumoto, 1997: 95).

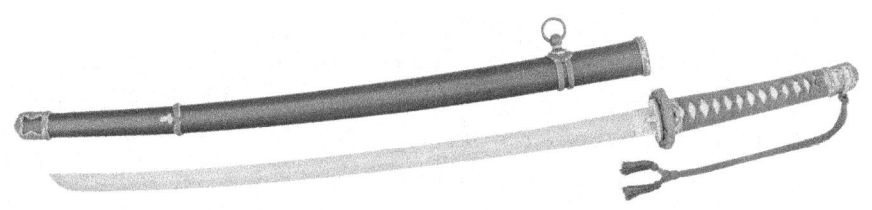

This picture shows a recreation of a *gunto*, which is the name commonly given to the swords carried by Japanese soldiers in World War II.

Although the culture of the nihonto is somewhat different from that of the Western European sword, it cannot account for all of the differences in the preservation and reverence of the sword. Rather, there are several legal aspects as well. In general, one of the most important elements is the governmental protection of nihonto. The primary protection comes from the Agency for Cultural Affairs.

The Agency for Cultural Affairs

The Agency for Cultural Affairs (ACA) was formed following WWII as a way to preserve traditional Japanese culture in the wake of the massive destruction of the war (Agency, website: 5). One of the primary responsibilities of the ACA was creating the system of categorizing and managing cultural properties. That responsibility manifested itself through the list of "Cultural Properties of Japan." The list contains assets of Japanese history and culture deemed to be of the utmost importance and worthy of protection. It is divided into two categories: tangible and intangible cultural properties (Agency, website: 2).

Tangible cultural properties are temples, shrines, residences, castles, crafts, and archeological artifacts. These items are further subdivided based on their relative importance. They are either categorized as "highly important" or "national treasures" (Agency, website: 4). Currently there are 110 swords and twelve sets of sword mountings on the list of registered national treasures (Wikipedia, National Treasures). In addition to tangible cultural assets, sword making is among the original crafts listed a "highly important" intangible cultural asset. People, as well as crafts, can be deemed intangible cultural assets. Colloquially called "living national treasures," these individuals have mastered the crafts considered fundamental to Japanese culture (Agency, website: 10). Any individual named a living national treasure receives an annual government grant to continue his or her craft. There are currently three individuals who fall under the category of sword making on the list, and there have been a total of ten individuals named living national treasures for their work with swords (Wikipedia, National Treasures).

The closest organization that could be compared with the ACA in the United States would be the National Park Service. Although both are tasked with preserving important culture and icons throughout the country, there are significant differences. The first and most important is likely the lack of a list of tangible cultural properties in the United States. There are several lists, such as the National Register of Historic Places, but none of them includes privately owned objects (16 U.S.C. 470). In addition, the protections that the Japanese place upon items listed as national treasures are far more restrictive than those in the United States (Agency, website: 5).

The general administration of the nihonto aspects of the list of cultural properties is left up to a separate organization, the Nihon Bijutsu Token Hozon Kyokai (NBTHK). The NBTHK is not a government organization, but is an authorized foundation, and it determines whether items are considered "highly important" or "national treasures" under the definitions set forth by the ACA (Nihon Bujutsu, website).

This *Tori katana* is made by CAS Hanwei in a similar fashion as a traditional nihonto, but is available for a fraction of the price. The cost difference is in part due to the artificial demand created by the Japanese culture and government. The value of a nihonto is not the extrinsic value of a well-made sword, but rather the intrinsic value of their artistry, history, and culture.

The Nihon Bijutsu Token Hozon Kyokai

Immediately following World War II, the United States occupied Japan. During this occupation, there was a universal ban on weapons, and this included nihonto. The servicemen of the United States occupation force destroyed or removed over half a million Japanese swords during this time. As a response to this assault on their traditions, the Japanese formed the Nihon Bijutsu Token Hozon Kyokai (NBTHK).

The NBTHK is the Society for the Preservation of Japanese Art Swords. As described, the Japanese truly feel that the swords are a traditional part of Japanese culture and are works of art, but it was difficult for the United States occupation force to understand the significance. In response, the NBTHK was founded to create an ambassador to the occupation force and attempt to stop the destruction of traditional Japanese weapons (NBTHK European, website).

This was not a strategy unique to the weapons themselves, but was also utilized in the practice of traditional sword arts, as well as other traditional martial arts. The suffix generally affixed to martial arts was *–jutsu*, which means "technique." During the occupation, the native practitioners began to refer to their arts with the suffix *–do*, which means "way." Thus, *kenjutsu* (the technique of the sword) became *kendo* (the way of the sword), and *jujutsu* (the gentle technique) became *judo* (the gentle way). By changing the names of the traditional arts of their culture, the Japanese managed to prevent the occupational forces from destroying some of most important aspects of their history (Ratti and Westbrook, 1991: 24).

Today, the NBTHK has eight primary activities and services (NBTHK European, website):

1) **The Conservation Project of Japanese Art Swords:** The NBTHK will issue certificates and registrations to swords, as well as give them a class. The classes are *hozon token* (worthy of preservation or authentic), *tokubetsu hozon token* (high quality and worthy of preservation), *juyo token* (historically important and authentic), or *tokubetsu juyo hozon* (historically important as well as high quality).

2) **Shinshakuto Exhibition:** *Shinshakuto* are newly made swords, and this exhibition is presented each year to show the best swordsmiths' work. Each year swords are awarded first, second, and third place, as well as *nyusen*, which means they were accepted to the competition. All the swords accepted to the competition are shown in the NBTHK museum. Swords are judged solely on their artistic value.

3) **Sword Polishing and Furniture Competition:** Similar to the forging competition, swords polishers and mounters are judged on the quality of their work.

4) **Tamahagane Smelter:** The NBTHK operates the smelter from which all swordsmiths receive their raw iron.

5) **Seminars:** Seminars in all of the traditional crafts surrounding sword making are given each year.

6) **Education:** The NBTHK offers classes for individuals interested in learning more about the artistic value of swords and how to value them. They also operate the Nihonto Museum in Tokyo.

7) **Magazine:** The NBTHK publishes a monthly magazine dedicated to the nihonto.

8) **Subsidies:** The NBTHK awards subsidies to those who practice the traditional crafting of Japanese swords to continue the tradition of excellence.

The most important responsibilities of the NBTHK are the shinshakuto competition and the conservation project. The shinshakuto competition gives basis for the awards given through the ACA, and the conservation project allows for swords to be given the required papers (*origami*) that legally make them into artwork.

Registering Nihonto

Although guns and swords are substantially different, especially in a Japanese context, they are both weapons and are generally regarded under the same or similar statutes. The primary statute for the possession of swords falls under the Act for Controlling the Possession of Firearms or Swords and Other Such Weapons (Act for Controlling, website). In most circumstances, it is illegal to possess either swords or guns in Japan, but there are various exceptions (Act for Controlling, website).

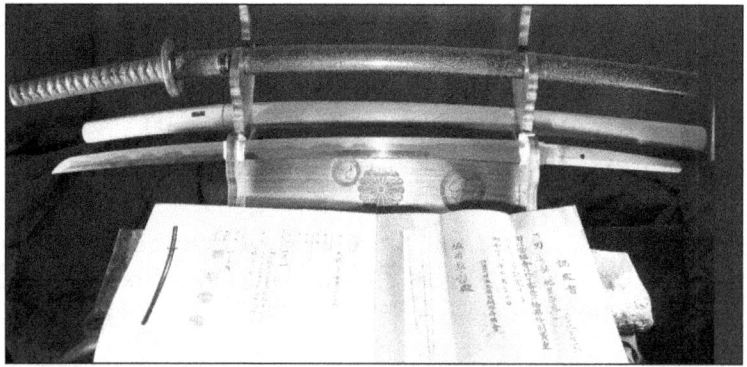

This is a photograph of an authentic nihonto from the early 17th century. This blade is a "first generation" sword (*shodai*) from the Hizen smithing tradition. Below the blade you can see the traditional origami that must be included for a sword to be owned, transported, or imported to Japan.

The primary exceptions allow for weapons to be possessed if they are used for "applications such as hunting, eradication of noxious birds and animals, slaughter of animals, fishing or construction, cases where possession is unavoidable due to Japanese customs and practice, cases where possession is unavoidable for plays or other artistic performances, and cases where such items are used for display in museums" (Act for Controlling, website, 4[2]i). In addition, weapons may be possessed if they have artistic or antique value (Act for Controlling, website, 4[2]i). The second exception is where most Japanese citizens find their right to have nihonto.

In order for a Japanese citizen to own a sword that is exempted for the reason of artistic or antique value, he or she must have it registered with the local prefecture board of education (Act for Controlling, website, [2]). The ACA is a special body of the Japanese Ministry of Education (Agency, website, 1). Since the ACA utilizes the NBTHK to determine which swords are of artistic value, a petitioner must prove to the prefecture board of education that the sword he or she possesses is registered with the NBTHK, generally with origami presented to the owner after appraisal.

In the end, through the creation of the NBTHK and laws of registration, a very effective form of weapon registration was created that did not demean the historical importance of the nihonto. The Japanese have always felt that the nihonto is an important part of their culture, but the U.S. occupational forces were very strict about the kinds of weapons that could be owned by individuals. By putting these protections in place the NBTHK created an effective compromise for both parties. In fact, in traditional Japanese fashion, it made the owners of the swords feel as though registration were both an honor and a duty, because their nihonto were of important historical significance.

The closest direct comparison in the United States would be the National Firearms Act (NFA) (26 U.S.C. ch. 53). The NFA also designates that certain kinds of weapons must be registered with the federal government, but there are substantial differences between the two acts. In the United States, most firearms laws are determined by the states (26 U.S.C. ch. 53). Sword laws are almost non-existent. The NFA only requires registration of a few kinds of weapons, mostly those that have caused problems with law enforcement in the past (26 U.S.C. ch. 53). While the real reason for the two acts may be the same, the sword section of the Japanese act seems to be written more as a way of preserving culture rather than a way of protecting the public.

The act is one of the strongest ways the Japanese have preserved their martial heritage. While it may seem as though requiring the registration and limiting the ability to own a sword would make them scarcer, it has had the opposite effect. Because the Japanese go to such effort to obtain and own these weapons, they have greater incentive to preserve them. In addition, the act provides for a centralized listing of all of the swords, allowing for greater government control and better records of those swords that do still exist.

Importing Nihonto

There are no specific laws about the importing of nihonto, but certain statutes work together to make it impossible to import a non-Japanese blade. The first statute of note is within the act. Section 25 states that a person may not enter Japan with a sword. If a person does, the sword will be confiscated until it is proven to be legal within the country (personal interview with Kazuyo Fujimura, Nov. 16, 2011).

In order for a sword to be legal within the country, as mentioned previously, it must be licensed with the prefecture board of education and have origami issued by the NBTHK (Act at 2). Under this definition, swords are only those made of steel (Act at 4[2]i). In Japan there are many "swords" sold in tourist locations or to practitioners of iaido. These swords, called *mogito*, are generally made of zinc aluminum alloy, and there is no restriction for entering or exiting the country with them (Schiller, website).

The final piece comes from the act itself, which states that "[t]he registration of swords is available for swords which are valuable as works of art, however only Japanese swords have been examined" (Act at 4[2]i). In this case, only a sword that has been registered may be brought into the country. These statutes continue to emphasize the perceived importance and superiority of the nihonto.

Because only nihonto may be kept in Japan, and because the Japanese have such a rich culture of swordsmanship, nihonto remain intact for generations. The only swords available to swordsmen and collectors in Japan are nihonto. Not only that, but the intense regulation of the manufacture of these swords makes them very rare, meaning that antique nihonto are incredibly valuable.

Manufacturing Nihonto

All swords in Japan must be registered, and the registration may only be granted to art swords of Japanese manufacture (Act at 4[2]i). Therefore, all newly made swords, *shinshakuto*, must meet the stringent guidelines of traditional Japanese sword manufacturing, which are enforced by the NBTHK (NBTHK European, website). This creates an effective monopoly on all swordsmithing within Japan.

While the guidelines were originally put in place to encourage tradition, they have created an artificial demand for nihonto that is continuously monitored by the NBTHK. The smiths must follow manufacturing guidelines, the most limiting of which is the use of officially licensed *tamahagane* (NBTHK European, website). The smiths may apply for this tamahagane from the NBTHK, which makes the iron in its smelter. It is the only raw material allowed for manufacture of a true shinshakuto (NBTHK European, website). If a sword is not made out of tamahagane, it will be destroyed immediately (Yoshindo, 1987).

This effectively limits the number of smiths capable of operating within Japan. In addition, the NBTHK limits the number of swords that may be produced. Japanese smiths may only make two swords per month, limiting them to twenty-four per year (Yoshindo, 1987). This is rumored to have been made a rule because the greatest swordsmith of all time, Masamune, took two weeks to make a quality sword. Whether that is true is still up for debate (Yoshindo, 1987: 30).

This artificial monopoly creates great demand for nihonto. Currently, in the United States, if a person wishes to purchase a Japanese styled sword, made by a smith (often trained in Japan), the asking price is between $2,000 and $5,000. If a person wishes to get a Japanese styled sword made in Japan, the asking price is generally at least $10,000 (and if it is made by a renowned smith or is an especially beautiful piece, prices can tip the scales to over $100,000). In addition, the wait time for a shinshakuto is generally between six months and two years, depending on the smith. Swords made in the United States are generally of the same quality, but lack the pedigree and origami of a true nihonto.

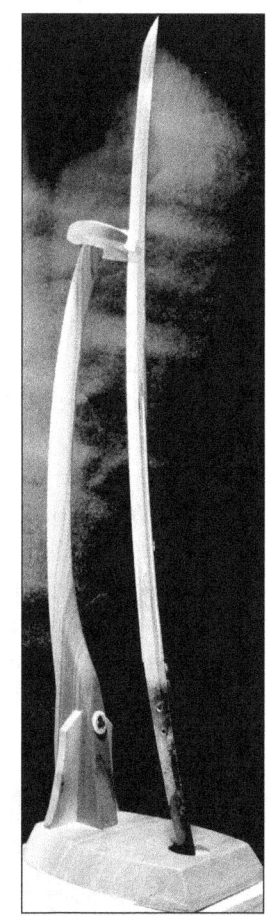

Whether or not the NBTHK made these rules as a means to achieve their goals of preservation is unknown, but they have achieved them. With these rules, the value of antique nihonto has skyrocketed, since people have such limited access to newly made pieces. With such high value, the Japanese have worked hard to preserve the swords that they already own, and thus, the NBTHK's goals have been realized.

This beautiful nihonto blade shows some of the defining characteristics sought after by collectors, including a *horimono* or blade carving. This particular sword is of the Mihara School and was likely forged between 1350 and 1500.

Conclusion

The Japanese have functionally created a monopoly around one of their greatest cultural assets. The word monopoly is a loaded term, but in this situation, it is not morally objectionable for this monopoly to exist. Although the Japanese have limited importation, manufacture, sale, and possession of this cultural commodity, it has worked to their advantage. Today there are more Japanese swords in excellent condition than any other kind of sword. They are collected, traded, and sought after. This intrinsic value, created by both culture and law, has led to a forced preservation. The governmental concern for this archaic art form has only strengthened the market. By creating this artificial demand, it has led to the conservation of one of Japan's greatest historical assets.

Acknowledgment

A special thanks to Ms. Kazuyo Fujimura, who helped with Japanese translations and statutory interpretations. Photographs of modern replica swords and the forging process were supplied by CAS Hanwei. The photographs of genuine nihonto are courtesy of Mr. James Rosch and are pieces from his personal collection. All photos are property of CAS Hanwei or Mr. James Rosch.

References

Act for Controlling the Possession of Firearms or Swords and Other Such Weapons. Translation available at: http://www8.cao.go.jp/kisei-kaikaku/oto/otodb/english/houseido/hou/lh_05050.html

Agency for Cultural Affairs, Cultural Properties for Future Generations: Outline of the Cultural Administration of Japan (pamphlet), available at http://www.bunka.go.jp/bunkazai/pamphlet/pdf/pamphlet_en_03_ver03.pdf

Encyclopedia Britannica, Definition: Sword available at: http://www.britannica.com/EBchecked/topic/577385/swordNihon Bujutsu Hozon Token Kyokai Homepage, available at http://www.touken.or.jp/english/index.html

NBTHK American Homepage available at: http://www.nbthk-ab.org/Japan.htm

NBTHK European Branch Homepage available at: http://www.nbthk.net/NBTHKe/NBTHK.html

Nihon Bujutsu Hozon Token Kyokai Homepage, available at http://www.

touken.or.jp/english/index.html

Oakeshott, E. (2007). *Records of the medieval sword*. Rochester, NY: Boydell Press.

Ratti, O. and Westbrook, A. (1991). *Secrets of the samurai: The martial arts of feudal Japan*. Edison, NJ: Castle Books.

Sayers, A. Introduction to Civil War cavalry. Available at: http://ehistory.osu.edu/uscw/features/regimental/cavalry.cfm

Schiller, G. The Japanese sword law. Available at: http://www.una.edu/faculty/takeuchi/DrT_Jpn_Culture_files/Nihon_to_files/SwordLawLetter.htm

Suino, N. (2001). *The art of Japanese swordsmanship: A manual of Eishin-ryu Iaido*. NY: Weatherhill Publishing.

United States Code, (1966). Volume 16, United States Code Section 470.

Wikipedia (n.d.). List of National Treasures of Japan available at: http://en.wikipedia.org/wiki/List_of_National_Treasures_of_Japan_%28crafts-swords%29 (Translated list available from the ACA's database, available at: http://www.bunka.go.jp/bsys/index.asp)

Yoshihara, Y. (1987). *The craft of the Japanese sword*. New York: Kondasha International.

Yumoto, J. (1997). *The samurai sword*. Tokyo: Charles E. Tuttle Publishing.

index

Agency for Cultural Affairs, 43-44
All American Karate Association, 4
All-Japan Karate Championship, 3
Amateur Athletic Union, 4
American Amateur Karate Federation, 5
American Independent Taekwondo/Karate Instructors Federation, 6
American Taekwondo Association, 6
art collectors, 42
Best of the Best (movie), 25
Black Karate Federation, 6
Black Book, The, 5
business consultants, 18, 21
Chow, William, 4
Crouching Tiger, Hidden Dragon (movie), 25
Demura, Fumio, 4
Draeger, Donald, 2-3
Enter the Dragon (movie), 25
Federation of All Japan Karate-do Organizations, 2
Funakoshi, Gichin, 2-3
globalization, 14-15, 24-28, 30, 32
Goju-kai, 2
Haines, Bruce, 4
iaido, 41, 48
iaijutsu, 41
International Judo Federation, 26
International Olympic Committee, 5
International Taekwando Federation, 6
International Traditional Karate Federation, 5
International Wushu Federation, 27
Japan Karate Association, 2
judo, 4, 14, 25-26, 28, 45
jujutsu, 45
Karate Kid (movie), 6, 25, 27
kendo, 41, 45
kenjutsu, 41, 45

Kosho-ryu Kempo, 4
Kung Fu (TV series), 25
Kyokushinkai, 3
Last Samurai (movie), 27
Lee, Bruce, 6, 25
management principles, 13, 15, 18-19, 21, 24, 28-31, 34
marketing strategies, 3, 5, 13-21, 27, 31, 34
martial arts schools, 13, 15, 18, 21, 23
Martial Arts America, 6
Martial Arts Sourcebook, 5
membership contracts, 6-8, 18
Midwest-based American Karate Association, 4
militaria categorization, 42
Mitose, James, 4
national chains, 6
National Collegiate Athletic Association, 4
National Firearms Act, 47
national treasure, 38, 43-44
Nihon Bijutsu Token Hozon Kyokai, 44-49
nihonto, 37-39, 41-44, 46-49
Nihonto Museum, 46
North American Sport Karate Association, 6, 8
Ochiai, Hidy, 10
Oyama, Masutatsu, 3, 11 note 3, 25
Parker, Ed, 4
Power Rangers (TV series/movies), 6
Professional Karate Association, 6
Professional Karate League, 6
promotion companies, 7
Rembo-kai, 2
Rengo-kai, 2
Rhee, Jhoon, 4
Shoto-kai, 2
Shotokan, 2, 4

Society for the Preservation of Japanese Art
    Swords, 44
sportification, 1-2, 7-8, 10, 14, 27-28
sword furniture, 39
sword registration, 38, 45, 47-48
Taebo, 27
taekwondo, 5-7, 14-16, 25-26, 28
Taekwondo Park, 26
Teenage Mutant Ninja Turtles
    (TV series/movies), 6
Tomita Shumeshiro, 25
tourist swords (mogito), 48
tournaments, 3, 6, 8-9
traditional iron (tamahagane), 40, 49
Trias, Robert, 4
U.S. Air Force, 3
U.S. Karate Association, 4
U.S. Karate Incorporated, 5
U.S. Olympic Committee, 4-5
U.S. Taekwondo Union, 6
U.S. Track and Field Federation, 4
United Fighting Arts Federation, 6
USA National Karate-do Federation, 5
Urban, Peter, 4-5, 10
Wado-kai, 2
World Taekwondo Federation, 6, 14, 26
World Taekwondo Union, 6
World Union of Karate-do, 5
World War II, 25, 37, 41-44
wushu/gongfu, 26-28
Yamaguchi, Gogen, 2-3
Yamaguchi, Gosei, 10
Yamashita, Yoshiaki, 25

www.ingramcontent.com/pod-product-compliance
Lightning Source LLC
Chambersburg PA
CBHW070119110526
44587CB00015BA/2648